DISCOVERING OUR HERITAGE

SPAIN

GATEWAY TO EUROPE

BY GERALDINE WOODS

DILLON PRESS
PARSIPPANY, NEW JERSEY

Acknowledgments

The author thanks Silvia Defior, Mariano Moles, Vanesa Moles, and Vital Moles for their help with this book.

Photo Credits

(Photo credits from previous edition)
The photographs are reproduced through the courtesy of the Carmel Mission Gift Shop; Collection, The Museum of Modern Art, New York, Mrs. Simon Guggenheim Fund, Pablo Picasso, *Three Musicians*, 1921 (summer), oil on canvas, 6'7" x 7'3-3/4" (200.7 x 222.9 cm.); Robert Fried (Copyright 1987, pages 8, 42, 103, 111, 117, 125, 138); Milt and Joan Mann—Cameramann International (Copyright 1987, pages 27, 112, 123); the National Tourist Office of Spain; Roger and Cowan, Inc.; Robert Royal—Creative Edge Photography (Copyright 1987, pages 38, 100, 121); Royce Carlton, Inc.; Tom Stack and Associates—Steve Elmore (Copyright 1987, page 85); UPI/Bettmann Newsphotos, page 64.

(Second edition photo credits)
Front Cover: Tony Stone Images/Cris Haigh: *l.* The Stock Market/Claudia Parks: *m.*; Darrell Jones: *r.*
Courtesy, Consulado General de España: 28. Odyssey Productions/Robert Frerck: 19. Tony Stone Images/Hugh Sitton: 72–73. Silver Burdett Ginn: 5. Courtesy, Tourist Office of Spain: 21, 37, 44, 45, 51, 82, 93, 127; Frank Shiell: 97. Map, Ortelius Design: 6.

Every effort has been made to locate the original sources. If any errors or omissions have occurred, corrections will be made.

Library of Congress Cataloging-in-Publication Data

Woods, Geraldine.
   Spain: gateway to Europe / by Geraldine Woods. — 2nd ed.
      p. cm. — (Discovering our heritage)
   Includes bibliographical references and index.
   Summary: Contrasts Spain's past of castles, Moorish invaders, and fair ladies with today's fast-growing democracy, featuring such cultural aspects as schools, sports, food, and folktales.
   ISBN 0-382-39767-3 (LSB)
   1. Spain—Juvenile literature. [1. Spain.]   I. Title. II. Series.
DP17.W59 1998
946.083—dc21   96-36996

Copyright © 1998 by Geraldine Woods
Cover and book design by Michelle Farinella

Published by Dillon Press
A Division of Simon & Schuster
299 Jefferson Road, Parsippany, NJ 07054

Second Edition
Printed in the United States of America
10 9 8 7 6 5 4 3 2 1

CONTENTS

Fast Facts About Spain

Official Name: *Estado Español*

Capital: Madrid

Location: Western Europe. Spain occupies most of the Iberian Peninsula and includes the Canary and Balearic Islands. Portugal is to the west and France to the northeast. To the north is the North Atlantic Ocean and the Bay of Biscay, and to the south and east is the Mediterranean Sea.

Area: 194,890 square miles (about 504,750 square kilometers). Spain extends 646 miles (1,040 kilometers) from east to west, and 547 miles (880 kilometers) from north to south. It has 2,345 miles (3,774 kilometers) of coastline.

Elevation: *Highest*—The Mulhacén, in the Sierra Nevada, 11,411 feet (3,478 meters) above sea level. *Lowest*—Sea level along the coast

Population: 39,347,000 (1996 estimated) *Distribution*—81 percent urban, 19 percent rural. *Density*—202 persons per square mile (about 81 per square kilometer)

Form of Government: Parliamentary monarchy. The king is the head of state, but the prime minister is the head of the government.

Some Important Products: Cars, ships, leather, chemicals, cement, steel, shoes, clothing; oranges, wheat, olives, lemons, oats, rye, wool, grapes; sherry, other wines

Basic Unit of Money: Peseta

Languages: Castilian Spanish, Catalan, Galician, Euskera (Basque), Valencian, and Majorcan are co-official languages.

Religion: Spain is 95 percent Roman Catholic.

Flag: Three horizontal panels of red, gold, and red, with the national coat of arms in the center gold panel

National Anthem: "Himno Nacional" (National Anthem)

Some Major Holidays: Catholic feasts of Christmas (December 25); Day of the Three Kings (January 6); Holy Week (the week leading up to Easter, date varies); many individual saints' days; New Year's Day (January 1); Students' Day (January 28) and Hispanic Day (October 12)

Spanish Provinces: Spain is divided into 50 provinces, which are grouped into 17 "autonomous regions." These regions share power with the central government.

THE HIDE OF A BULL

Mention "Spain" and most people immediately imagine a ferocious bull, charging a matador who is whirling gracefully behind a red cape. *Corridas*, or bullfights, are probably Spain's most famous tradition. In one form or another they have been associated with Spain for centuries. So it is fitting that the name of the country itself, Espana, comes from a Latin word for "the hide of a bull." The third largest country in Europe, Spain occupies most of the Iberian Peninsula, a nearly square block of land at the western edge of Europe. Portugal lies along the Atlantic coast of the peninsula, and France borders northeastern Spain. The ancient Romans, who once ruled these countries, thought that the shape of the peninsula was similar to that of a cattle skin stretched out to dry. The Latin word for this skin, "Hispania," became the name of the province and eventually, España.

To the north of this "hide" is the North Atlantic and the Bay of Biscay, and to the south is the Mediterranean Sea. Two groups of islands are also part of Spain. The Balearic Islands lie in the Mediterranean Sea to the east of the Spanish mainland. They consist of five large islands and a number of smaller ones. Majorca, Minorca, and Ibiza are the three largest Balearics. The 13 Canary Islands are in the

The dry plateau called the Meseta stretches across most of the Iberian Peninsula.

Atlantic Ocean about 60 miles from northwest Africa. The Canary Islands form two separate Spanish provinces.

Most of the Iberian Peninsula is a high, flat plateau called the Meseta, or "little table." Seen from the air, the Meseta is a rolling patchwork in thousands of shades of brown and gold with only small patches of green. On this plateau, the flat areas are not very fertile and are divided by hills and mountains. The region's weather is sunny for

Spain's beautiful countryside includes plains, low hills, and mountains.

most of the year—pleasant for people, but very dry for farming. Summers are extremely hot on the Meseta, and despite the sun, winters are fairly cold.

Not all of Spain is dry, though. The wettest part of the country, Galicia, occupies the northwest corner of the peninsula. Before America was discovered, the Romans had named this area *Finisterre*—"the end of the earth." It rains in Galicia almost every day, and a fine, mysterious-looking mist covers the ground on many mornings. Galicia has many green fields and long stretches of marshlands.

Cutting through the Meseta are several mountain chains called *sierras*, a word meaning "saws." The Sierra Morena, Sierra Nevada, and Sierra de Guardarrama are the most important. Spain's highest peak, the Mulhacén, is located in the Sierra Nevada. The Galician, Cantabrian, and Pyrenees mountain ranges run across the northern edge of Spain. Spain has so many mountains that its average altitude is second in Europe only to that of Switzerland. The Meseta is also crisscrossed by a number of important rivers, including the Guadalquivir, the Ebro, the Duero, the Tajo, and the Guadiana. These rivers supply much of the water used for irrigating crops in regions bordering the Meseta.

Spain is famous throughout the world for its Mediterranean coastline. The *Costa del Sol*, or "coast of the sun," and *Costa Blanca*, or "white coast," are located in

Several rugged mountain ranges cut through the Meseta.

southern Spain. Clean, sandy beaches and sparkling weather there attract many visitors. The *Costa Brava*, or "fierce coast," is also an appropriate title for the shoreline along the Mediterranean near France. Here, high cliffs and jagged rocks lie next to a sparkling blue sea.

An Isolated Nation

A few years ago a campaign to attract tourists to Spain used the slogan "Spain is different." More than 100 years earlier, the Emperor Napoleon of France put it another way when he said, "Europe ends at the Pyrenees." Although both statements are exaggerations, each is partly true. Spain's customs, history, and attitudes have traditionally been very different from those of other European countries.

This difference may be due to Spain's geography, which is full of natural barriers. Only 300 miles of border link Spain to the rest of the European continent, and the rugged Pyrenees Mountains lie along the entire length of that border. Spain's other mountain ranges run between coastal areas and the interior Meseta. Also, many Spanish rivers, because of rapids or low water levels, cannot be used by large ships. Before modern methods of travel were invented, it was hard for Spaniards to travel out of their country and for foreigners to enter it. Aside from the waves of invaders that pierced the country's defenses from time to time, Spain remained apart from the rest of the continent throughout its history.

Spain's mountain barriers also helped to isolate one region of the country from another. Many Spaniards refer to their nation as "my Spain"—a sign of the personal pride they feel for their country. However, most Spaniards don't personally think of themselves as Spaniards. Instead, they identify themselves by the particular area in which they were born. They sometimes refer to this area as their *patria chica*, "little homeland."

Most of these patria chicas were independent kingdoms at some point in Spanish history. These traditional
regions of Spain each developed distinct ways of living.
Through the years they were forged into one nation, divided
into provinces, and later grouped into larger units called
autonomous (self-governing) regions. The creation of
autonomous regions is one way Spain has chosen to deal
with the desire of people in many areas to separate themselves from the central government. By sharing power with
local authorities, the government has balanced national
unity with regional identity. However, the autonomous
regions are still fairly new, and many Spaniards ignore
them in everyday speech. For example, if a native of
Salamanca is asked where he or she comes from, the
answer will probably not be "Castile-Léon," the name of
the autonomous region formed in 1981. Instead, the reply
is likely to be "Old Castile," the name of the kingdom
formed during the Middle Ages.

Two Castiles, Old and New, both traditional regions,
give their name to the most widely used language of Spain,
Castilian. Castilian is easy to recognize because the letters
c and *z* are often pronounced as if they were *th*'s. In Latin
American and other forms of Spanish, *c*'s and *z*'s are pronounced as *s*'s. (See appendix A for a guide to pronounc-
ing Castilian Spanish.)

Both Old and New Castile are located on the Meseta,

and with the help of irrigation, the area has become an important agricultural region. Because Madrid, the capital and largest city of Spain, is located in New Castile, the area is also a major business center. Almost all of Spain's large companies and banks, as well as many foreign businesses, have headquarters or branches in Madrid. The city's broad avenues are lined with modern office buildings and government centers.

Modern Madrid is quite different from the sleepy little town King Philip II found when he moved his capital there in 1561. King Philip thought that Madrid's location in the center of the country would help unify Spain. Another king, Ferdinand VII, founded Madrid's Prado Museum. Today the Prado is one of the greatest art museums in the world. Still another king, Juan Carlos I, now lives in Madrid in the Zarzuela Palace. The Royal Palace, also in Madrid, is used for state functions. It is one of the most amazing buildings in the world. It has 2,800 rooms and is surrounded by a stately, formal garden.

A short drive from Madrid is Ávila. Although Ávila has thriving wool and tanning (leather) industries, it is more famous for its historic sites. Ávila was built in the Middle Ages. At that time, it was surrounded by a thick stone wall to protect its residents from attack. The wall still exists; people who live in Ávila can easily imagine that nine hundred years of history have just rolled away and a

*Modern Madrid is the largest city of Spain
and a major business center.*

knight in shining armor is about to ride through the city.

Citizens of Segovia, a city near Ávila, can imagine they are in an even earlier era. In Segovia is an ancient aqueduct, which brought water from the mountains. This system for transporting water was built by the Romans in the first century A.D. The Romans were such good builders that the stone blocks of the aqueduct stay together without cement or mortar! In the Middle Ages, Segovia was the center of the Spanish textile industry. Today it relies on tourism as a main source of income.

Basque province. The city has great iron and steel-making plants and is an inland seaport on the Nervión River.

Both the Catalonians and the Basques have their own language, although most people also speak Castilian. For many years the central government in Madrid outlawed the use of the Catalan and Euskera (Basque) languages to encourage ties with the rest of the country. The government was afraid that these provinces would rebel and break away from Spain to become independent nations. Both areas have always had strong independence movements.

The creation of autonomous regions has given the Catalans and Basques much more power to govern themselves. The Catalan and Euskera languages are again permitted and even encouraged. However, some people in these regions still favor complete independence. A few have turned to terrorism to achieve this goal. In the last 25 years, Basque terrorists have killed over 750 people in an attempt to further their cause of separation from Spain. In 1995, investigators discovered that some officials of the central government had organized "death squads"— special agents who hunted and killed Basque terrorists. The special agents, as well as the officials who directed them, were themselves put on trial for murder. The scandal toppled the ruling socialist government in 1996.

The region of Asturias is ringed by rugged mountains

that separate it from the rest of the peninsula. This isolation may have encouraged the fierce independence for which the region is known. During the eighth century, when Moors from Africa took control of the Iberian Peninsula, Asturias was one of the few areas that they could not conquer. The mountains of Asturias are the richest coal-mining region in Spain; the area also contains deposits of iron, zinc, lead, and copper. Recently plans were made to reopen a gold mine originally dug by ancient Romans! Oviedo, the region's leading city, is an industrial center with many factories producing steel, glass, chemicals, and processed food.

Galicia, in northwestern Spain, also has its own language. Its coastline has many good harbors, and the area supplies one third of the nation's fish. Almost 30 percent of Spain's cattle are raised in Galicia. However, Galicia has poor soil and little industry. During the 1900s about a million and a half Galicians emigrated to Latin America, the United States, and other parts of Spain.

While praising their own part of Spain, many Spaniards criticize (somewhat jokingly) the rest of the nation. These criticisms often take the form of comments about the reputations of the natives of a particular area. For example, many Spaniards will tell you that a typical Andalusian is happy-go-lucky and somewhat lazy. The word *mañana*, or "tomorrow," sums up this view of

Andalusians. When they say "mañana," they mean "never do anything today that you can possibly put off until tomorrow." Aragonese people are said to have heads so hard and thick (stubborn) that they can hammer nails with them! A typical Galician is often considered poetic, superstitious, and musical; a Castilian is often assumed to be proud. Spaniards sometimes say that Catalonians worship *"Don Dinero"* (Sir Money) and that they could "squeeze bread out of a stone." As for the Basque provinces, there's a story about the time the devil hid behind the door of a Basque house because he wanted to learn to speak Euskera. However, after a year of listening, the only words he knew were "Yes, ma'am." The story shows how difficult other Spaniards consider Euskera—and how strong they consider Basque women! The language part, at least, is probably true. Not many can pronounce this Basque name: Barrenecheagamechucoicoecheaiturri.

Agriculture and Industry

Although Spain has traditionally been an agricultural country, its farmers have always faced several serious problems. The soil is very poor in most parts of the peninsula, and expensive fertilizers must be used to produce good crops. The land is also very dry, although a network of irrigation canals helps provide water in many areas.

Heavy investment in modern machinery has also helped increase crop yields, but human effort can only go so far. Mother Nature remains a powerful force. In the early 1990s, Spain experienced a five-year drought, the worst in living memory. Farmers found themselves fighting luxury tourist hotels for the supply of water. Although recent rainfall has helped, Spanish farmers still cannot produce enough food for the entire nation, and Spain must buy what it needs from other countries. The drive to conserve water has become an important issue for Spain's growing environmental movement.

Spain's main cereal crops are wheat and barley. Fruits such as grapes, oranges, lemons, and melons are also grown. The area around Valencia is known for its oranges, rice, and sugar harvests. Andalusia is lined with olive groves; sunflower plants are also grown there, and the seeds are used to make cooking oil. Sheep, goats, and other animals are raised throughout Spain, particularly where the soil does not support crops.

In recent years, the number of Spaniards working in industry has increased at a tremendous rate. The government is still trying to encourage the development of new manufacturing and service businesses in Spain. At present, Spain's most important products include cars, ships, steel, cement, chemicals, clothing, and shoes. Fishing is a major source of income in Galicia and the areas that border on the

Spain is a leading producer of olives.

North Atlantic. Tourism is another important nationwide industry. Each year thousands of people flock to "sunny Spain" for vacations.

Unemployment is a major problem in Spain today. The country lacks many minerals, and its industries must import raw materials. This cuts down on profits and limits the number of workers businesses can hire. Agricultural workers are also affected; there are simply more people available than jobs. To make matters worse, some of the work in farming is seasonal. Many hands are needed at harvest time, but few are employed during the winter months.

Developing new industry is important to Spain.
This man works in electronics.

As a result of all these factors, unemployment has risen above 20 percent in recent years . This means that one out of every five workers is unable to find a job. The rate is even higher for Spaniards under 25 years of age.

Governing the Country

Spain is a parliamentary monarchy. King Juan Carlos I is the head of state and also the commander of the armed forces. The king does not have absolute power. Juan Carlos

King Juan Carlos I and Queen Sofía (center) *with their children, Princess Elena, Prince Felipe, and Princess Cristina*

cannot command his subjects or order the government to obey. He can propose new laws and approve laws passed by the country's lawmakers. He may declare war and sign peace treaties and appoint or dismiss high government officials in accordance with the results of elections. King Juan Carlos' most important power, however, does not come from the constitution. He is greatly respected by the Spanish people, and, therefore, his views often influence government decisions.

The head of the government is the prime minister, who is the leader of the political party that controls the most seats in Parliament. The prime minister works with a Cabinet to run the government day-to-day. At present, Spain has many political parties, including the Popular Party, the Socialist Workers' Party, the Communist Party, and the Democratic Coalition.

Spain's Parliament, the Cortes, has two houses. The upper house is called the Senate and has 208 members. The Chamber of Deputies, or lower house, has 350 members. Spanish citizens elect representatives to both houses of the Cortes every four years. As does the United States Congress, the Spanish Parliament makes laws, approves treaties, and sets tax rates.

The 17 autonomous regions, like Spain as a whole, are democracies. Citizens elect delegates to local and regional assemblies, which pass laws concerning local matters. The exact distribution of powers between the central government and the autonomous regions is still being worked out. In general, the autonomous regions function as state governments in the United States do.

As we have seen, the regional assemblies preside over areas with very different geography, customs, and character. Nevertheless, all of Spain's regions also share common bonds, most of them forged during the long history of the peninsula and its people.

THE ARTS IN SPAIN

Once upon a time a man lived in the center of Spain in a region called La Mancha. He was of noble birth, but his family had fallen on hard times and he was now extremely poor. The man was very old, and his bones tended to creak when he moved. Therefore, he spent most of his time in the house, reading books about the glorious days of knights and their code of honor called chivalry.

By and by, his brain became confused. Although the age of chivalry had ended centuries before, the man began to believe that he was a knight. He found a rusty suit of ancient armor, a broken-down old nag of a horse, and a fat little peasant, Sancho Panza, for a squire. Lastly, he adopted a new name: Don Quixote de la Mancha. Then he rode out into the countryside to save people and fight for justice.

Many of Don Quixote's adventures were comical. For instance, he attacked a windmill, convinced that it was a giant waving its arms. Don Quixote wasn't just a clown, however. His belief in a beautiful, magical world and his idea that one should fight for what is right influenced people. Because Don Quixote was a good person, he made everyone around him better.

Don Quixote never really lived. He is a character in one of the most famous books in the world, *Don Quixote de la Mancha.* This novel was written in 1605 by Miguel de Cervantes, a writer whose life was almost as exciting as his writing. (Cervantes was wounded in battle, made a slave, captured by pirates, and later arrested after his escape!) Don Quixote does live, though, in the hearts of Spaniards. That's because he shows many of the human qualities most respected in Spain.

First of all, Don Quixote is a true gentleman. He has perfect manners, but his manners are not just on the surface. They come from a deep sense of honor. The Spanish idea of honor calls for demanding the respect due you as well as taking full responsibility for your own actions. A professor at the University of Madrid once showed his sense of honor when he arranged an overnight field trip for his students. Because of a mix-up in the hotel reservations, there were not enough rooms for everyone. Although he was nearly 80, the professor insisted on giving up his room to a student. He spent the night on the bus. "A gentleman cannot rest when those he is responsible for are uncomfortable," he explained.

Don Quixote is also an idealist; he believes that a perfect world is possible, and he often tries to achieve what everyone else considers impossible. Many scholars have observed this same habit in Spanish history—in the 1930s constitution, for example, which tried to reform every aspect of Spanish life. The effort failed, but it was a courageous try.

Macho Man

Don Juan is another important imaginary figure in Spain. Don Juan is a character in many of the world's great plays, poems, and operas. He was created in the seventeenth century by a Spanish playwright named Tirso de Molina. Don Juan is a handsome man who attracts the attention of women wherever he goes. He is, however, also heartless. His habit is to win a girl's love and then abandon her after a few days. In Tirso de Molina's version, Don Juan pays dearly for this behavior. He challenges the statue of a dead man to a duel and dies when the ghost returns to fight him. At the end of the play, the ghost takes Don Juan to eternal punishment.

A few centuries later, José Zorilla was kinder to Don Juan in the play he wrote. Although he is just as evil in this version, Don Juan is loved by a very saintly woman. Her prayers are enough to save him. Don Juan has a change of heart and ascends to heaven with her when he dies. Because of its hopeful ending, this play is often performed on All Souls' Day, November 2, the feast day on which Catholics pray for the souls of the dead.

Like Don Quixote, Don Juan is popular because he expresses some ideas that are widely accepted in Spain. Although no one believes that abandoning women is the right thing to do, many Spaniards admire that Don Juan is strong and clearly in charge where women are concerned.

These qualities are summed up with one word: *macho*. A macho or "manly" man doesn't help with the dishes; that's women's work. He whistles or whispers compliments when he passes a pretty woman on the street. He alone decides what is best for his family, and he expects his wife to go along with his ideas. For many years, Spanish law backed up this custom. As late as 1975 the Civil Code said, "The husband must protect his wife and she must obey her husband." Without her husband's agreement a wife could not get a job, start a business, open a bank account, or sign a contract.

Until recently, law and custom kept most Spanish women in very sheltered lives. They remained in the home, cooking, cleaning, and caring for their husbands and children. Few women held outside jobs, unless the income was absolutely necessary for the family. As many Spanish men respected Don Juan, many Spanish women looked up to the saintly woman who saved him. They admired her holiness and her willingness to devote herself to the man she loved.

But things are changing. In 1976 the first feminist demonstration in Spain was held. Only 2,000 women marched, but the timing was right. Improving the rights of women became part of a larger crusade for freedom that gripped Spain after its elderly dictator, Francisco Franco, died. Spanish laws soon included a guarantee of equal rights for women. In the 1980s, Spanish women flooded into the universities. By 1987 more than half the country's college students were female. In 1988 the Spanish army was opened to women. Although the numbers are still low, women now hold positions in the highest levels of government, law, and business.

In the home, some Spanish women are also achieving greater equality. Such women consider themselves full partners in family decisions and expect their husbands to share in the work at home. However, the struggle for women's rights is far from over in Spain. Many families still follow the traditional roles. In many families the mother is still responsible for child care and housekeeping, even if she holds a full-time job outside the home. Women's salaries are, on average, lower than those of men, and women have a higher rate of unemployment than their male colleagues.

A Streak of Sadness

Federico García Lorca, another famous Spanish writer, also captured part of his nation's soul in his writing. García Lorca was born in Granada in 1898. He often wrote poems about the South of Spain, and much of his writing is very sad. In one of his poems, for example, he speaks of the city of Córdoba as "far away and alone." A rider is traveling to Córdoba on a black horse, but Death is watching, and the rider knows he will never get there. Federico García Lorca may have had a feeling about his own future when he wrote this poem. A few months later, during the Spanish Civil War, he was shot while in prison.

Although Spaniards love parties and can be very merry, the sadness of García Lorca's poem is also a part of the Spanish character—perhaps because life on the Iberian Peninsula has never been easy. The harsh climate, the poverty, and the wars in Spain's history have given Spaniards reason to mourn. The work of Spain's most famous modern novelist, Nobel prize winner Camilio Jose Cela, also reflects this sadness.

The traditional music of Spanish gypsies, flamenco, also has a sad quality. Flamenco music is played on a guitar and is accompanied by singing, hand-clapping, and foot-stamping. Dancers whirl to flamenco music, clicking little wooden shells called castanets and tapping out the dance's rhythm with sturdy shoes. Although the beat appears lively, most flamenco songs are about lost love, poverty, and unhappiness. One type of flamenco music is the *solea*. A typical solea describes a poor family working long hours in the fields. Although they dream of buying their own farm one day, they know they will never achieve their goal. Flamenco has been updated by the addition of pop, salsa, and American blues. The recordings of the "new flamenco" stars—Ketama, Rosario Flores, and Pata Negra—have brought a new generation of fans to the form.

Of course, not all Spanish music is sad; *zarzuelas* are actually joyous! Zarzuelas are plays set to music. The actors sing and dance throughout the performance and occasionally speak a few lines of dialogue. The stories are usually funny and romantic.

In addition to flamenco and the zarzuela, each region of Spain also has its own folk music. In Galicia, where the Celts from Ireland invaded long ago, musicians often play the bagpipe, and dancers' steps resemble those of the Irish jig. In Aragon, the *jota* has long been popular, and in Catalonia, people traditionally have danced the *sardana*. These dances are often performed outside. In Barcelona on Sunday mornings, the main plaza fills with hundreds of dancers and musicians. The dancers join hands and move gracefully to a slow beat.

One custom popular in all the provinces of Spain involves a *tuna*. A tuna is a small singing group made up of young men, usually from the same university. Members of the tuna wear clothes patterned after sixteenth-century styles: short, full pants; black stockings; short jackets; and long, full capes. The tuna traditionally serenades a pretty girl. The singers stand in the street as the young lady sits on her balcony. When the songs are finished, the girl throws colorful ribbons to the musicians. The members of

Dancers perform a traditional dance, the jota,
at a local fiesta.

the tuna pin the ribbons onto their capes. They often have whole rainbows of ribbons on their clothing!

Spain can also boast of some musicians who are famous the world over. Andrés Segovia—who was born in Linares, in 1893, and died in 1987—is considered the father of the Modern classical guitar movement. He invented a method for playing classical pieces on the guitar that created a whole new type of music. Alicia de Larrocha, who plays classical music on the piano, also performs internationally. Placido Domingo, Victoria de los Angeles,

Jose Carreras, and Montserrat Caballe are world-famous opera singers.

The Art of Spain

If you travel on Spain's national airline, Iberia, it's possible to fly on a jet named "El Greco." El Greco was a master painter who worked in Spain in the sixteenth century. His name means "the Greek," indicating where he was born. "Domenikos Theotokopoulos," his actual name, was too hard for Spaniards to pronounce! Nevertheless, he lived most of his life in Spain and is considered a Spanish painter. The fact that the airline chose to name one of its planes after an artist shows how much Spaniards respect art.

El Greco's paintings have an unusual style. They often show people with long, sad faces, and they are painted in unnatural colors with many patches of shadow and light. Diego Velázquez, on the other hand, painted more realistically. He lived in the seventeenth century and was the official court painter for King Philip IV. One of his most famous pictures shows the tiny princess Margarita Teresa and her maids of honor. The dwarf who entertained the royalty at court, the princess's pet dog, the king and queen, and even Velázquez himself are in the picture.

Another great Spanish artist, Francisco Goya, was born in 1746. Goya also painted portraits of royalty, but he

Members of a tuna stroll through the streets, stopping to serenade a young lady.

was not always kind to his subjects. If Goya did not like a king or queen, he painted every wrinkle and ugly feature, exactly as he saw it. Goya is also famous for a series of drawings called *The Disasters of War*, which shows terrible scenes of suffering and death during the nineteenth century Spanish revolt against the French rulers.

A more recent Spanish master, Pablo Picasso, also criticized violence by means of his art. Picasso was born in Málaga in 1881. He was one of the first painters to produce cubist art—a style in which shapes such as squares, circles, and triangles are used to represent people and objects. Although Picasso spent much of his adult life in France, he often used Spanish themes in his work. One of his most famous drawings, for example, is of Don Quixote and his helper Sancho Panza. Another canvas, *Guernica*, shows a Spanish tragedy. During the Spanish Civil War, after German bombers destroyed the Basque city of Guernica, Picasso created the huge painting to show the agony caused by the bombing. In *Guernica*, a mother holds her dead baby. The mother's head is shaped like a screaming mouth, and her eyes have turned into tears.

Pablo Picasso died in 1973, but the great tradition of Spanish art continues. Some art experts estimate that there are about five hundred internationally known Spanish artists working today. One of these is Antonio López García, a painter and sculptor of wood. López García is a

Pablo Picasso was a pioneer in modern art. His painting
Three Musicians *(1921) is an example of cubism.*

patient man—one of his pictures of Madrid took 8 years to create, and another took 20 years! Another contemporary artist, Miguel Barceló, creates pictures with paint and such objects as string, paper strips, and cigarette butts. Eduardo Chillida and Susan Solano are noted sculptors. A Spanish dress designer once turned some of Chillida's sculptures into clothing. Models paraded on the runway in the striking geometric designs.

This street artist carries on Spain's rich creative tradition.

Today, Spain has about 2,500 art galleries that often feature the work of new and unknown artists as well as the pictures painted by well-known artists. That's a huge number of galleries for such a small country! Spain also has many internationally renowned art museums, from the stately Prado in Madrid to the ultra-modern Museum of Contemporary Art in Barcelona. Along with the many Spanish writers, dancers, and musicians, Spain's painters share their nation's love of self-expression and continue its rich creative tradition.

SPAIN'S CHANGING FACE

Over 13,000 years ago, one of the world's first artists entered a cave deep inside a hill in northern Spain. The artist lay down on a broad, flat, stone close to the roof of the cave. Within easy reach were several sea shells to use as drawing tools, each containing a different color. "Paint" was made of dark brown, tan, and reddish bits of dirt or charcoal, mixed with grease and cork. With strong, sure strokes, the artist sketched a number of animals on the white limestone ceiling and walls of the cave—bulls, deer, bear, and wild boar.

Many years passed, and the artist's people died or moved away. Natural forces in the earth changed the shape of the land. Huge boulders closed off the entrance to the cave. Air and moisture, which might have damaged the paintings, were nearly sealed out.

The drawings were in almost perfect condition in 1879, when a young Spanish girl named Maria de Sautuola found a crack in the rock and looked through it. At home she told her father about the marvelous pictures she had seen inside Altamira cave. Although we still can only make guesses about who drew the pictures, and why, Altamira has become famous throughout the world as one of the best examples of prehistoric art.

*Cave paintings of animals may have been an attempt
to capture the creature's spirit.*

The Altamira pictures are extremely old, but even so,
they are not the work of the earliest Spaniards. Historians
believe that human beings first arrived on the Iberian
Peninsula over 100,000 years ago. Little remains from that
long period of unrecorded history, although archaeologists
have found some stone tools and a number of dolmens in
addition to the cave paintings. Dolmens are small buildings
made of slabs of rock. They were probably used as tombs.

The prehistoric tribes who built these structures are not
the only ancestors of present-day Spaniards. Time after
time, Spain has experienced waves of immigration and

This stone monument was built by the ancient ancestors of present-day Spaniards.

invasion from other countries. The Iberians walked into the country from northern Africa around 3000 B.C. At that time, Europe and Africa were connected by a land bridge that later submerged and finally became the Strait of Gibraltar. The Iberians gave their name to the peninsula. They settled along the Ebro River. ("Ebro" comes from the Iberian word *iber*, which means "river.") These people built Spain's first cities, and two of their settlements, Tarragona and Cartagena, are still in existence today.

The Iberians were fierce fighters who erected strong walls around their cities to protect themselves. Their artists decorated vases with pictures of warriors fighting on foot, on horseback, and from the decks of small boats. The Iberians also crafted delicate gold pins, bracelets, and necklaces. They created many bronze statues of bulls, other animals, and flowers. The most famous remaining artwork of the Iberians is a stone statue of a young woman. Since she was found near the town of Elche, she is called "The Lady of Elche." The "Lady" wears many pieces of jewelry and a huge headdress. She may have existed as an Iberian princess.

Around 1200 B.C. another people, the Phoenicians, arrived in Spain. The Phoenicians came from the Middle East. Although they founded the cities of Cádiz and Málaga, the Phoenicians were not really interested in maintaining colonies in Spain. They were a trading nation—they wanted the silver, gold, copper, lead, and other minerals of western Spain.

Another wave of people entered Spain in 900 B.C. and again in 600 B.C. These immigrants were the Celts, the same ethnic group that populated Ireland, Scotland, and Wales. The Celts settled in northern Spain. As they spread southward, the Celts often found themselves at war with the Iberians. In time, however, the Celts and the Iberians intermarried, and a new ethnic group was formed—the Celtiberians. Around 600 B.C. the Greeks traveled to Spain to trade with the Celtiberians. The Greeks established a number of settlements, but like the Phoenicians, they were not interested in forming permanent colonies.

The inhabitants of Carthage, on the other hand, did conquer large sections of Spain. Carthage was a Phoenician city in North Africa, located near the site of modern-day Tunis, Tunisia. Around 300 B.C., Hamilcar Barca, a Carthaginian leader, founded Barcelona. Barca's son Hannibal conquered all of Spain south of the Ebro River. Hannibal also attempted to defeat the mighty Roman Empire and is remembered for using elephants in his war on Rome. Although he won some important battles, in the end Hannibal was not successful. In fact, Roman troops attacked Carthaginian armies in Spain and eventually drove the Carthaginians out of the Iberian Peninsula entirely.

The Roman Era

Roman soldiers began to fight the Carthaginians and native Spanish tribes for control of Spain in the third century B.C. Two hundred years passed before the Romans had gained complete control over the peninsula. Because of their fierce courage, the Spaniards became famous throughout the empire. In fact one whole legion of Roman troops revolted when they found out they were being sent to fight in Spain! Once the war was over, however, the

Romans constructed many buildings like this theater at Mérida during their rule.

people of Iberia settled down to a long period of peace. Spain became Hispania, a Roman province.

The Romans made many contributions to Spain during the almost four centuries they ruled there. They founded or enlarged 800 cities and crisscrossed the province with roads. They built theaters, bridges, arenas, and aqueducts to carry water. The Romans also introduced Christianity to

Hispania in the first century A.D. By 325, almost everyone in Spain was a member of the Christian faith. The Roman language, Latin, also spread throughout the land. (Today, four of the five main languages of the Iberian Peninsula—Spanish, Portuguese, Galician, and Catalan—are based on Latin.) The common language and religion, as well as the strong Roman government, changed the small separate tribes of the peninsula into a united group.

In return, Hispania supplied Rome with minerals, livestock, and food crops. At one point, Hispania was the wealthiest province of the entire empire. Three Roman emperors, Trajan, Hadrian, and Theodosius, were born there. Several famous Roman authors, including Seneca, Lucan, and Martial, also came from Hispania.

When the Roman Empire crumbled in the fifth century, the same Germanic tribes that overran Italy invaded the Iberian Peninsula as well. One of these tribes, the Visigoths, conquered all of Hispania in 573. The Visigoths greatly admired the Romans, whose empire they had helped to destroy. Their nobles soon adopted Spanish customs, language, and religion. However, the Visigoths proved to be poor governors; during their reign the strong central government of the Roman era began to break down, and the country split into tiny kingdoms. At one point, there were more than 30 Visigothic kings in Spain, most of whom were squabbling with their neighbors!

The Moors

Because of this weakness, it was relatively easy for Sheik Tarik Aben Zyad (the One-Eyed) to lead an army of Moors from Morocco in North Africa to Spain in 711. His landing place was named "Tarik's Rock" in his honor. (In Arabic this is *jebel Tarik*, which eventually became "Gibraltar.") Tarik was followed by thousands of other Arabs. By 718, all of the Iberian Peninsula, except for a small strip of land across the northern coast, was controlled by Arabs.

The Arabs were Muslims, or followers of the religion of Islam. Although they had conquered Spain in honor of their God, Allah, they allowed the native Spaniards to practice their own religions. In the 700 years that they were in Spain, the Moors made many contributions to Spanish culture. They constructed hundreds of beautiful palaces, castles, and mosques. Arab scholars also brought advanced knowledge of medicine, astronomy, and mathematics to Spain. One Arab ruler, Abd-al-Rahman I, introduced new farming methods into southern Spain. With the help of irrigation, Spanish farmers began to grow banana trees, sugar cane, cotton, and date palms during his reign. Abd-al-Rahman also promoted silk weaving, paper making, and leather crafts. His artisans became skilled in a type of elaborate metal decoration called damascene work, which is still done in Spain today.

This building in Seville shows the Moorish influence on Spanish Architecture.

The Reconquest

Although the Arabs remained in Spain until the fifteenth century, their control of the peninsula was often challenged. The native Spaniards revolted frequently. One important battle occurred in 722. In that year a Spanish chieftain named Pelayo gathered his followers in a cave called Covadonga in northern Spain. The Arab army sent to defeat Pelayo failed. Even so, the Arab rulers did not consider Pelayo important enough to challenge with another attack. No harm could come from such a small band of warriors, they reasoned.

They were wrong. Through the years, Pelayo became a symbol of Spanish resistance, and his kingdom, Asturias, became the starting point of the Spaniards' rebellion against their Arab conquerors. The period of time between the battle of Covadonga and the final defeat of the Moors in 1492 is called "the Reconquest" by Spanish historians. During this 700-year period, native Spaniards won land from the Arabs, piece by tiny piece. As each area came under Spanish control again, the conquerors formed new kingdoms. These Christian kingdoms, eager to expand their power, often went to war with each other. In addition, the Arab states of Spain often quarreled among themselves. So the inhabitants of Spain saw every form of war during the long period of Arab rule—Spaniard against Arab, Spaniard against Spaniard, and Arab against Arab.

woman, was raised to believe that nothing was more important than religion. Ferdinand was a courageous soldier. He and Isabella followed their armies from battle to battle; several of the couple's ten children were born in military camps. Ferdinand and Isabella ruled Spain as powerful partners. In fact, their royal motto was "Isabella is the equal of Ferdinand."

To Ferdinand and Isabella, the effort to drive the Moors from Spain was a religious crusade. They wanted all of their subjects to follow the Catholic faith. To achieve this goal, Ferdinand and Isabella also established the Inquisition in 1480. It was to operate for about 300 years. The Inquisition was a religious court with unlimited power to imprison, torture, and kill anyone suspected of not believing in Catholic teachings. Protestants, Jews, and Muslims were often arrested. Catholics whose faith seemed different from that of the established religion were also tried by the Inquisition. Those convicted of heresy were usually given three choices: to change religions, to die, or to leave Spain. Over 2,000 Spaniards, most of them innocent, were executed by the Inquisition. About 150,000 people fled to other European or African countries. In 1992, King Juan Carlos marked the 500th annniversary of the Inquisition by praying at a Jewish temple, thereby condemning hatred and lack of respect for other religions.

The Inquisition also banned those books it considered

dangerous to the Catholic faith. To find such books, a simple test was used. The Inquisition believed that books that were truly holy would not burn, so texts accused of being antireligious were thrown into a fire. Needless to say, this test proved the Inquisition's suspicions correct again and again.

Though people today view the Inquisition as shameful, the reign of Ferdinand and Isabella was also marked by great achievements. In 1492, Isabella agreed to finance an expedition to find a water route to Asia. The captain, Christopher Columbus, never reached the Far East. However, the New World he found more than made up for this failure!

The Spanish Empire

During the fifteenth and sixteenth centuries, many Spanish explorers were drawn to the Americas. Vasco Núñez de Balboa led an expedition across Panama and became the first European to see the eastern reaches of the Pacific Ocean. Hernán Cortés conquered the mighty Aztec Empire of Mexico, and Francisco Pizarro claimed Peru, where the Inca people lived, for Spain. Juan Ponce de León explored what is today the state of Florida; Hernando De Soto, Álvar Núñez Cabeza de Vaca, and Francisco Vásquez de Coronado were the first Europeans to travel

The conquistador Hernán Cortés conquered much of central and southern Mexico, including the Aztec Empire.

through what is now the southern United States.

These *conquistadores*, or "conquerors," claimed vast amounts of land for Spain. Of course, all of this territory was already home to the North and South American Indians. In the Spaniards' view, claiming these lands and possessions was not stealing, and even killing or enslaving the native people was acceptable behavior.

At the same time, Spanish conquistadores invaded and won territory in North Africa and parts of Europe. Soon a vast Spanish Empire was formed. At its height, the empire included Mexico, California, the American Southwest, half of South America, Portugal, and parts of North Africa, France, Italy, Belgium, and the Netherlands. The last two areas had been ruled by a grandson of Ferdinand and Isabella, Charles I. Charles was a Hapsburg, a member of the royal family that was to rule Spain for almost 200 years.

This huge empire brought Spain tremendous wealth. Gold, silver, and other treasures from the Americas poured into Spain. The nation seemed to be riding a wave of success. Even Spanish artists and writers felt the effects; the sixteenth and seventeenth centuries are known as Spain's "Golden Age" because of the great literature and art produced during this period.

However, even as the wave of success reached its crest, situations that would eventually destroy the empire were developing. First of all, conquering other countries is very costly. Each war drained Spain of men and money. Many Spanish colonies revolted against their rulers, resulting in more wars, more lost lives, and more expense. In addition, the government made a number of extremely unwise laws. Each Spanish shoemaker, for example, was allowed to make only certain styles of shoes, limiting each one's customers greatly. Also, wealth from the colonies did not reach the common people of Spain. The country had many poor peasants and a few tremendously rich people who made up the ruling class. Not surprisingly, many Spaniards decided to leave their homeland to seek their fortunes in the New World. Since many Jews and Moriscos (Arabs who had converted to the Catholic religion) had already been expelled by the Inquisition, Spain had a shortage of workers, and the economy suffered.

The year 1588 marked the beginning of the end of the Spanish Empire. In that year, King Philip II decided to send a mighty force of Spanish ships to fight England. The fleet was called the Armada, and Philip expected an easy victory over the English. Instead, poor weather, lack of supplies, and unwise military decisions brought defeat to Spain. After 1588 the empire lost territory in a series of wars. By the late seventeenth century, many of the European lands Spain had conquered were gone. France even controlled parts of Spain itself. When the Spanish King Charles II died without an heir, a Frenchman, Philip of Anjou, took the throne as Philip V. This touched off yet another long and costly war among several European nations. This "War of Spanish Succession" ended in 1714. All the rest of Spain's possessions in Europe were taken away. Philip V was allowed to keep his throne; the line of kings he began was called the Bourbons.

The Bourbons ruled for about 100 years. Then in 1808 Napoleon Bonaparte, the French emperor, seized control of Spain's government and put his brother on the throne of Spain. Joseph Bonaparte was hated by the Spaniards. People called him *Pepe Botellas* ("Joe Bottles") because they considered him a drunkard. The discontented Spaniards drove Napoleon out after five years of hit-and-run, guerilla warfare. The Spanish kings returned to the throne, but they were not to remain there for long.

Early in the nineteenth century, Spaniards who wanted more rights for the Spanish people and a limit to royal power wrote a constitution. The rulers of the time, however, would not allow it to be put into effect. Throughout the century, there were constant quarrels between supporters of the constitution and supporters of the monarchy. To make matters worse, those who favored a royal government also disagreed among themselves. When Ferdinand VII died in 1833, some Spaniards wanted his daughter Isabella to rule. Others, who were called Carlists, supported Ferdinand's eldest brother, Carlos. Isabella became queen, but the Carlists were never satisfied with her.

In the last years of the nineteenth century, there was great unrest in Spain. Spain's last foreign colonies, Cuba and the Philippines, were taken away after the Spanish-American War of 1898, a five-month war with the United States. The military revolted, the monarchy was exiled and then returned, and a republic was established for a brief period. (In a republic, laws are made by representatives of the people.) In 1923 an army general named Miguel Primo de Rivera led a revolution. King Alfonso XIII, knowing he had no real choice, supported the revolution. Primo de Rivera became prime minister, but he had the powers of a dictator. He ruled until 1930, when the army overthrew the government. Finally, in 1931, general elections were held in Spain. The people voted overwhelmingly in favor of a republic. Alfonso XIII fled the country, and there was great rejoicing throughout Spain. "We have had a revolution without spilling a single drop of blood!" the people exclaimed.

The Republic and Civil War

These words came back to haunt Spain only a few years later, for the Republic was doomed to fail. Everyone who supported the Republic agreed that conditions in Spain had to change. Unfortunately, that was the only thing they agreed on. Land reform is a good example. The

Republic passed a law breaking up some huge estates so that land could be distributed to the peasants. The law was immediately attacked—both by those who thought it was too strong and by those who thought it was too weak. Each side formed a political party and tried to gain power in the government. Spain ended up with too many political parties, all fighting each other, each gaining and losing power almost daily. In four-and-a-half years of republican government, Spain had 26 major political crises and 72 different ministers in its government.

The Republic also tried to accomplish more than was possible. It once passed a law requiring that all Spanish children attend school. At the time the law was passed, however, there were only enough schools to accept one quarter of the nation's students!

Another explosive issue was the role of the Catholic Church in Spain. Since the days of the Inquisition, the Catholic religion had been almost the only faith in Spain. The Church owned huge amounts of land and was closely tied to the ruling classes. When the Republic began its reforms, it often clashed with the Church. Some angry radicals who supported these reforms attacked priests and nuns and burned church property. This upset many sincerely religious Spaniards and made them enemies of the Republic.

In July 1936 General Francisco Franco felt compelled

to take action. Born in the city of El Ferrol, Galicia, in 1892, Franco attended a military academy in Toledo and then rose quickly in the Spanish army. Serving for many years in Morocco, he was a respected leader. In 1936 he became Chief of Staff of the Army of the Spanish Republic. However, he soon found he disagreed with the policies of the government. In the spring of 1936, he was ordered to the Canary Islands. When he secretly left the Canary Islands for Morocco, he committed an act of treason. But he would go even further—he would return to the mainland from Morocco to begin the Spanish Civil War.

The Spanish Civil War was one of the bloodiest wars in history. On one side were Franco, other army officers, the church, and all those who believed in a government ruled by a single, strong person. They were known as the Nationalists. Franco's forces received troops, money, planes, and weapons from the dictators of Italy and Germany, Benito Mussolini and Adolf Hitler. On the other side were the Republicans and an assortment of political parties that wanted more power for individual Spaniards. They were aided by Russia and by thousands of people around the world who viewed the Spanish Civil War as a struggle for democracy. Some Republican supporters sent money and supplies. Others actually came to Spain to fight. A large group calling itself the Abraham Lincoln Brigade arrived from the United States.

Generalíssimo Francisco Franco led the Nationalist Army
during the Spanish Civil War. In this 1936 photograph,
he reviews some of his troops.

The war was fought from town to town for three long years, until General Franco triumphed in 1939. By the end of the Civil War, over 640,000 Spaniards were dead; 400,000 were in exile; and 2,000,000 were in jail. Spain had suffered more than 12 billion dollars in damage. Just about every family in Spain had lost a relative, friend, or home to the war.

The Franco Years and the Future

During the war, General Franco had taken the title of *Generalíssimo*, or "supreme commander." In 1939 the Generalíssimo organized what he called a "temporary" government to bring the country back to normal. This temporary government lasted almost 40 years, until Franco's death in 1975.

Spaniards who lived through the Franco years are divided in their opinion of him. Many older people who remember the horrors of the Civil War praise the Generalíssimo for bringing the country such a long period of peace. They also credit Franco with the improvement in living conditions. Although Spain has never been a rich country, it had one of the highest rates of economic growth in the world during the 1950s and 1960s. Businesses started and expanded at a fast pace. Under the Franco government, there were also many improvements in education, medical care, and transportation. Some Spaniards even jokingly referred to their leader as "Froggy Franco" because he opened so many new water projects to help the farmers.

Younger Spaniards, however, often point out that the benefits of Franco's rule carried a high price tag. "Generalíssimo" was really another name for dictator. Franco was the supreme ruler of the country. Though the Spanish Cortes continued to meet, it had no real power. Furthermore, representatives could be members of only one political party—Franco's. All other political parties were banned, as were trade unions, demonstrations, and newspapers that criticized the government.

Franco also chose his successor. Juan Carlos I, the Bourbon grandson of Alfonso XIII, grew up at Franco's side. Franco spent a great deal of time with the young prince, teaching him how to carry on the same type of government after Franco's death. On the surface, Juan Carlos appeared to believe in Franco's ideas. In public he said little, doing all that the old dictator requested. Secretly, however, Juan Carlos was convinced that democracy was the only system suitable for a modern nation. In the last years of Franco's life, Juan Carlos conferred secretly with political leaders sympathetic to change. Because Franco would have objected to these meetings, the politicians were smuggled into the prince's palace. One arrived inside the trunk of a car! Juan Carlos also installed a communications network in his palace that allowed him to speak to leaders all over the country within minutes.

Ordinary Spaniards knew none of this. When Franco died, many Spaniards doubted that the new king would be strong enough to hold the country together. They thought that Franco's death would trigger another civil war and referred to the king as "Juan Carlos the Brief." Yet only five days after taking power, the king granted a pardon to political prisoners. A short while later, he allowed free trade unions to form and lifted the ban on political parties. In 1977, Spain held its first free elections since the days of the Republic. In his first speech to the new Cortes, Juan Carlos announced, "Democracy has begun." Four years later, when civil guards and the army attempted a military takeover, Juan Carlos used his communications center to call military leaders around the country. He told the soldiers the same thing he told the entire nation later that night on television: Spaniards should have a voice in their government. Democracy would be destroyed, he said, "over [his] dead body." Because of the king's influence, the revolt failed.

Spain changed greatly during the first decades of Juan Carlos's reign. Besides becoming a democracy, the country also strengthened its ties with other European countries. Spain became a member of NATO (the North Atlantic

Treaty Organization), a defense organization that includes the United States and many European countries. Spain took a more active role in the United Nations, participating in UN peacekeeping missions and taking a turn on the Security Coucil. In 1991, Spain was host to a Middle Eastern peace conference and a summit meeting of Spanish-speaking countries. In 1992 the Olympic Games were held in Barcelona, Seville was the site of a world's fair (Expo), and Madrid was named "the European capital of culture."

In January 1986, Spain was admitted to the European Community, a trade group of European nations. Membership in the European Community brought many economic benefits to Spain. Investors sensed that the country, isolated during the Franco years and starved for the conveniences of modern life—televisions, VCRs, and the like—would be a great new market. Industry boomed, raising the standard of living quickly. During the last half of the 1980s, Spain's economy grew faster than that of any other European country.

In the early 1990s, however, the boom slowed. Spain now faces a new challenge. In a few years the European community will begin to use a common system of money. If Spain participates, its money will be the European Currency Unit (ECU), not the peseta. This new system will bring many advantages to members, increasing the speed of investment and trade. In order to use the ECU, how-ever, nations must meet certain economic standards. By 1996, Spain had satisfied only one of the five requirements. The country may have to make some painful changes in taxes and government benefits to achieve the other four.

Spain went a long way toward ending its cultural isolation during the 1980s and 1990s. Foreign movies, books, and art exhibits are now common in Spain; during the Franco years many of these cultural exchanges were banned by the government. Immigration has also broadened the country's outlook. At one time almost all the permanent residents of Spain had been born there. Now more and more Spaniards are originally from Africa, the Americas, or other European nations.

In the last two decades, Spain has also broken some of its traditional ties with the Catholic Church. Divorce, birth control, and some abortions (activities opposed by the Church) were made legal. Censorship was also abolished. For the first time in decades, Spaniards were allowed to question their government's policies. A number of new magazines and newspapers containing lively debates on political and social problems have been established.

Not every change has been welcomed. Some people believe that the new freedom has led to the breakdown of traditional Spanish values. These people point to a high number of AIDS cases, increased drug use, a rising crime rate, and a boom in pornography as the results of this breakdown. Others feel that new customs from America and other countries are overshadowing Spain's own culture. Video games and VCRs, for example, have encouraged more people to stay at home in the evenings—a time most Spaniards traditionally spent taking a walk or chatting in a café.

Still, Spain looks to the future. In 1986, Juan Carlos's son Felipe (Philip) was named "Prince of Asturias." According to Spanish custom, this title is given to the successor to the Spanish throne, in honor of Pelayo, the Asturian chief who began the Reconquest in 722. Although Felipe is young, most Spaniards admire him and look forward to his reign. What seems certain, however, is that democracy is now firmly established in Spain. The future King Felipe will be a limited monarch, much as Queen Elizabeth II is in Great Britain. He will be the most famous person in the next generation of Spaniards—a people whose history stretches back through the Civil War, the age of Columbus, the Roman Empire, and the coming of the Iberians, to the unknown artist who sketched a bull on the ceiling of Altamira cave.

THE ARABE DUCK AND OTHER TALES

When the Moors invaded Spain, a little duck came with them. This animal, whose name was Arabe Duck, was very hungry. However, he was also lazy and he did not like to hunt for his food as other animals did. So Arabe Duck went to the shore of a pond and said to an old crab who was resting there, "I can tell the future by looking at the stars. This pond will dry up soon. Gather all the fish for me, and I will carry them in my beak to another pond." Of course, Arabe Duck intended to eat the fish, not save them.

The crab was rather stupid, so he did what Arabe Duck wanted. But crabs have eyes in the backs of their heads. When the crab headed into the water, Arabe Duck thought the crab couldn't see him, but he was wrong. The crab saw the fish disappearing down Arabe Duck's throat.

The crab came back to Arabe Duck and said, "Bend your head, little duck, and I will hold it in my claw. Then you can carry me to another pond, too." Arabe Duck bent down, and the powerful claws of the crab caught him. That was the end of Arabe Duck!

Spanish children often hear the story of Arabe Duck. The story is typical of many Spanish folk tales because it

(Next two pages) *The Alhambra, built by the Moors, is said to house the ghosts of many warriors.*

(Inset) *According to Spanish stories, ghosts may walk this courtyard in the Alhambra when the moon is full.*

shows an Arab in a bad light. It seems that Spaniards, at least in their folk tales, have not forgiven the Moors for invading Spain centuries ago!

Even so, Spaniards continue to be fascinated by their enemies of long ago. Another story, "The Golden Pitcher," tells of a long-dead Moorish princess whose spirit is not allowed to rest. During her lifetime she had become a Christian, and her family had placed a curse on her. She was condemned to haunt a cave until a pure, kind Spanish girl agreed to hold her hand and pass through the trials of hell with her. Conchita, this poor peasant, finally helped the unhappy princess and received a golden pitcher as a reward.

The Spaniards also tell tales of Moorish ghosts who sleep in the Alhambra, once the Moors' palace in Granada. According to the stories, the ghosts of many warriors and of the last Arab king, Boabdil, wait for the day when they will awaken and reclaim Granada. Until that time, they may break their rest only when the moon is full. On those nights, they walk the courtyard of their ancient palace.

To Zaragoza or Back to the Pond

Some Spanish fairy tales poke fun at people from various regions in Spain. The Aragonese, for example, have a reputation throughout Spain for being stubborn. In one old

favor for a wasp. The wasp flies through the window and stings the Carlanco many times. The monster runs out of the house in pain and fright, and the goats are saved.

Coplas and Riddles

Animals appear in *coplas*, too—but then, just about everything appears in these short poems set to music. The oldest coplas were written centuries ago; the newest ones are being written right now, by any Spaniard who feels like making up a song. Mothers sing them as lullabies. Drivers make them up to pass time on the road. Workers sing them together, and farmers hum them in the fields. As one copla says:

> I have a little jug
> Of coplas and songs.
> When I want to enjoy myself
> I take the cork away,
> and the verses pour out!

Coplas can be funny:

> He that loves a woman
> Who doesn't love him
> Is the same as a bald man
> Who finds a comb in the street.

And coplas can be serious:

> What use is it to the prisoner
> To have bars of silver
> And chains of gold
> If he doesn't have freedom?

They can be written about children:

> This tiny baby
> Has no cradle.
> His father is a carpenter
> And will make him one.

And about adults:

> Take, girl, this orange;
> I give it to you because I love you.
> Don't cut it with a knife
> Because my heart is inside.

In other words, coplas can be about anything, by anyone, and sung anytime!

Another popular way to pass the time is to tell riddles. Can you guess the answers to these? (Look at the end of the chapter to see if you guessed right.)

1. We have two legs, but we can't go anywhere without a man, and he can't go anywhere without us. Where we?

2. What runs and runs and never arrives at its owner's
   house?
3. A thousand of us travel along one path, but we kick
   up no dust. Who are we?
4. I live on high, wearing a little golden crown. Even if
   the Moors come, I cannot run away. Who am I?

Like children all over the world, Spanish boys and
girls enjoy telling these riddles to each other. They also
love to hear traditional Spanish stories. In recent years,
however, the Smurfs, Mickey Mouse, and E.T. have
become popular in Spain as well. Little Arabe Duck and
the Carlanco have some new international friends!

(Answers: 1. pants, 2. a windmill, 3. ants, 4. an acorn)

A YEAR OF HOLIDAYS

A few minutes before midnight on December 31, people all over Spain make sure they have 12 grapes ready. In Madrid, huge crowds gather in La Puerta del Sol. La Puerta del Sol, "Gate of the Sun," is the city center. In other parts of the country, television sets are turned on. Everyone wants to see—either in person or on TV—the ball that drops at the exact moment the New Year begins. Most important, everyone wants to hear the huge clock of La Puerta del Sol chime the 12 strokes of midnight. At each stroke, Spaniards eat one grape: Swallowing all 12 before the clock stops chiming is said to bring luck during the coming year.

Five nights later, Spain celebrates again. January 6 is the Day of the Three Kings—the feast of Epiphany—which honors the Wise Men who traveled to Bethlehem to bring gifts to the infant Jesus. On the eve of the feast, there are joyous parades. People adorned as kings, angels, shepherds, and other figures from the Bible ride through the streets on floats. Little children watch in wonder and try to catch the candy the Kings throw to the crowd.

This probably is not the first time the Spanish children watching such a parade have seen the Wise Men. For weeks children have been visiting department stores with

their parents to see the Kings. Instead of telling Santa Claus what they want for Christmas, the children tell the Wise Men, and they receive their gifts on the Day of the Three Kings instead of on Christmas morning.

When the parade is over, the children put their shoes on the windowsill, along with a little bit of straw. In the morning they expect the shoes to be filled with toys. The straw is for the Wise Men's camels to eat!

Holy Week and *Feria*

A few months after the Day of the Three Kings, there is a more serious occasion. The week before Easter, Spaniards observe Holy Week. Holy Week serves to remind people of the death of Christ. In every city and town, there are religious processions. Often, in small villages, every single inhabitant joins in a solemn march behind a life-sized cross. A young man dressed as Christ carries the cross. He is guarded by other villagers costumed as Roman soldiers.

Some of the most impressive Holy Week ceremonies are in Seville. Each parish in the city mounts a float carrying a statue of the Virgin Mary. The statues are made of painted wood and are often very old. Parishioners donate jewels and money to make rich robes for each statue. One of the most famous statues is called *La Macarena*. Poor

Marchers in the traditional clothes usually worn at festivals

people and bullfighters believe that La Macarena takes
special care of them, and they often give her special
presents.

Although the floats can weigh up to a thousand pounds
each, they are carried by men from the parish. The floats
are surrounded by other parishioners dressed in long robes
and pointed caps—costumes like those worn by officers of
the Inquisition centuries ago. The marchers walk without
speaking, because they have taken a vow of silence. From
time to time, members of the crowd accompanying them
chant a short, sad song called a *saeta*. *Saeta* comes from
the Latin word for "arrow." The songs are "arrows of
prayer" shot into heaven.

During Holy Week just about everyone, even little
children, stays up late into the night. On Easter Day, everyone is tired. Most Spaniards attend religious services in
their parish churches and then spend a quiet day, visiting
with relatives and friends.

A few weeks after Easter, the people of Seville celebrate their city's *Feria*. The Feria is like a three-day party
for residents of the city and tourists alike. There are bullfights, circuses, carnivals, and parades of horseback riders.
Many families picnic in small, open tents outside the city.
While the adults feast on pastries and delicacies, children
dressed in flamenco costumes entertain them.

People prepare to parade these giant statues through the streets during a fiesta in Burgos.

Saint Joseph's Day, for example, carpenters might take a holiday and attend special ceremonies, since Saint Joseph was a carpenter. One day is celebrated by all workers. On July 18, employers are required to give their employees (in addition to their regular wages) half their monthly pay as a bonus. (They must make a similar payment at Christmas.) Students are honored on the feast of Saint Thomas Aquinas, a learned man. No one attends classes on that day, and many families cook special meals to please their own young scholars.

The Running of the Bulls

The Fiesta of San Fermin at Pamplona is one of the most famous and exciting in Spain. From July 7 through July 14, young men gather in Pamplona from all parts of Spain, and even from around the world. For one week each man wears his swiftest shoes, his loosest clothing, and his bravest smile. That week, bands begin to play throughout the city every morning at 5:45, and there is dancing and singing in the streets. A little later the young men gather in front of a large wooden corral on one side of the city. Inside the corral are bulls, each weighing over 1,000 pounds and each extremely dangerous.

Soon a rocket goes off and the corral is opened. The men begin to run, and so do the bulls! They follow a course between wooden barriers through the streets of Pamplona. All along the way, crowds watch from windows, balconies, and sidewalks. Since the bulls are just as frightened as the men they are chasing, few stop to charge the slower runners. Some men have been injured or even killed during the festival of San Fermin, however.

After a few minutes the runners arrive at their destination—Pamplona's bullring. The bulls are steered into a separate pen, and young cows are led into the ring. (The cows are used because they are less dangerous.) For the next hour or so, the runners get a chance to act out every Spanish child's dream. With a cape, or perhaps with just a jacket or a scarf, they tease the animals, thereby showing their own courage. They become bullfighters.

National Holidays

Many of the days on which schools and offices are closed are holy days of the Roman Catholic Church or are the feast days of saints. Corpus Christi (Christ the King), the Assumption of Mary, All Saints' Day, and the Feast of the Immaculate Conception are celebrated throughout Spain, as are Santiago (Saint James') Day and the saint's day of King Juan Carlos.

In the United States, October 12 is celebrated as Columbus Day. This is also a holiday in Spain, but it is called Hispanic Day. The nation honors its most famous explorer as well as its ties with Spanish-speaking countries around the world. In addition, October 12 is the feast of the Virgin del Pilar, one of the patron saints of Spain. So there is double reason to celebrate.

Christmas

By December, children all over Spain are already making up lists of gifts they want from the Three Kings. Recently some children have also begun to follow foreign customs. They write to Papa Noel (the Spanish version of Santa Claus), hoping that they will be given gifts on both Christmas and on the Day of the Three Kings! However, Christmas is not traditionally a day of presents and parties, as it is in the United States. The focus is on the religious meaning of the day.

Shortly before Christmas, most families display a *belén*—a nativity scene, complete with a stable, animals, straw, shepherds, wise men, and of course, Jesus, Mary, and Joseph. Some families buy ready-made stables, but in others, the children construct a homemade version using plastic figures, paper straw, foil stars, and perhaps a little cotton snow. Churches also have belenes during the Christmas season, and children sometimes dress in costume to make a living display in church.

On Christmas Eve, which is known as "The Good Night" in Spain, families gather around their belenes to sing Christmas carols. Later in the evening, many attend "The Rooster Mass." This religious ceremony begins at midnight, the first moment of Christmas morning. The mass gets its interesting name from the fact that roosters crow to signal the start of a new day.

Christmas Day itself is usually spent quietly, although family and friends often get together for a festive meal. Dessert is often a cake shaped like a fish, a symbol of faith. Children also eat candy made of marzipan (almond paste) and *turrón*, a hard candy traditionally served at Christmas. At this time of year, many families also serve a cake with a toy baked inside. The child who receives the piece of cake containing the toy is then named king or queen for the day.

There is one more holiday before another new year begins with 12 grapes and 12 strokes of the clock. On December 28, "The Day of the Innocents," Spanish children often play tricks on their elders. As on April Fools' Day in the United States, everyone must be careful on December 28. If someone borrows money, for example, he or she may remark, "May the Holy Innocents pay you ..." Of course, the sentence is easy to finish: "...because I won't!"

SPANIARDS AT HOME

A popular saying in Spain is that Spaniards "eat all day and some of the night." Of course, this isn't true—no one really eats *all* day. However, Spaniards do manage to scatter a lot of snacks and meals throughout each 24-hour period!

For adults the day begins, as it does in many countries, with a cup of coffee. Spanish coffee is *expresso*. Later in the day, Spaniards will have their coffee in tiny cups, because expresso is an extremely strong coffee, and a little goes a long way. Then, expresso can be taken *solo* (alone) or *cortado* (cut) with a spoonful of milk. But in the morning these beverages are too harsh for most Spaniards, so they use a large cup (almost like a bowl) and drink a half-and-half mixture of coffee and hot milk.

Many young children have hot chocolate instead of coffee for breakfast. Spanish hot chocolate is very thick, like a kind of soupy pudding. The perfect partner for this hot chocolate is a *churro*, a long, thin, fried doughnut that scoops up the chocolate as efficiently as a spoon. However, many people have just a piece of bread with their coffee or chocolate in the morning. This is more filling than it sounds, since Spanish bread is almost a meal in itself. The crust is very thick and crisp, and the inside is dense and tasty. Many Spaniards enjoy it so much

Churros are a favorite food for breakfast.

that they eat a piece with almost every meal.

Dinner is not until 2:00 P.M., but everyone is hungry by mid-morning, so Spaniards have a snack at about 11:00 A.M. Children eat their snack during their school recess; adults take a break from work. The most common snack is a *bocadillo* (little bite), but this treat is far from little. It's a roll stuffed with eggs, sausage, fried fish, or cheese.

Dinner (*comida*) is the main meal of the day. Traditionally schools, offices, and stores closed for a

Some Spanish houses are built around courtyards.

A seafood market in Madrid

Gazpacho

1 medium cucumber
1 small onion
1 clove garlic (1 piece from a whole bulb)
1 green bell pepper
3 large tomatoes
2 slices of day-old bread
2 cups water
2 tablespoons wine vinegar
1/4 teaspoon salt
2 tablespoons olive oil
1 tablespoon tomato paste

1. Peel the cucumber, the onion, and the garlic clove. Cut open the bell pepper and remove the seeds and stems. Crush the garlic clove with the back of a spoon. Chop the other three vegetables into one-inch pieces. Place all in a large bowl.

2. Chop the tomatoes into one-inch pieces and add to the bowl.

3. Crumble the bread into crumbs with your hands. Add to the vegetables.

4. Add the water, the vinegar, and the salt to the bowl and mix.

5. Using a blender or a food processor, blend all the ingredients until they are smooth. (Ask an adult to help you with this.) If there is too much for the machine, blend the soup in small batches.

6. Put the soup back in the bowl and add the olive oil and tomato paste. Blend well.

7. Refrigerate the soup at least two hours. Mix before serving.

Although it is not famous outside of Spain, the most popular dish on the peninsula is probably the *Tortilla Española*—an omelette of potatoes and eggs. This is how to make one.

Tortilla Española

1 medium-sized potato
3 eggs
1/8 teaspoon salt
olive oil

1. Peel the potato and cut it into half-inch cubes.
2. Break the eggs into a bowl, sprinkle with salt, and beat until they are completely scrambled.
3. Cover the bottom of a small frying pan with a thin film of olive oil. Heat the oil over medium heat for a minute. Add the potato cubes and cook them until they get soft, stirring occasionally.
4. Pour the eggs into the pan and cook until the bottom sets. Lift the edges of the tortilla (omelette) to let the liquid egg run off the top to the bottom.
5. When the bottom is lightly browned, slide the tortilla onto a plate and cover it with another plate. Turn the plates upside down and slide the tortilla back into the pan. Cook until the other side is firm and lightly browned.
6. Remove from the heat. The tortilla can be cut into wedges like a pie and served hot or cold. You can also put a piece inside a small roll to make a bocadillo.

Another famous dish from Spain is paella, a mixture of

Many Spaniards enjob paella, a mixture of seafood, meat, vegetables, and rice.

seafood, meat, vegetables, and rice. The rice is seasoned with a yellow spice called saffron. It is cooked in a wide, flat pan. When the paella is brought to the table, a plate of salad is placed in the middle of the pan. Diners begin at the edge of the pan and eat their way toward the middle—right from the pot. When the salad is done, the plate is removed and everyone finishes off the middle of the paella.

Here is a recipe for the hot chocolate that is a popular breakfast drink for children. Spanish hot chocolate is so thick that you may have to use a spoon to eat it!

The Church and Everyday Life

Almost everyone in Spain is Catholic, and the Church plays an important role in everyday life. All the major events in life—birth, marriage, and death—are marked by religious ceremonies. In fact, until the late 1970s the only marriage ceremony permitted in Spain was a Catholic one, and divorce was illegal. Now, Protestant, Jewish, Muslim, and other houses of worship exist in all major cities, and in many small towns as well.

Nevertheless, in most villages, the Catholic Church is an important social center. Children go there for religious instruction, to attend choir practice, and to meet in youth groups. Adults meet after services to exchange greetings with their neighbors; many also belong to church-sponsored clubs. The entire town may attend Sunday services. The children sit together in a special section.

Spaniards are generally named after saints. However, the saint's name is only the beginning. Spanish names follow a complicated pattern.

Let's take an imaginary child named Maria. Her mother's family name is Sanchez and her father's name is Díaz. Maria will have two last names, one from her father and one from her mother. The father's is written first, and if anyone is in a hurry the mother's is not used. So this child is called Maria Díaz Sanchez, or Maria Díaz for short.

Suppose Maria marries José Galdos Rodriguez when she grows up. He keeps his name, and she keeps her name. However, she may also be called *la señora de Galdos*—the wife of Galdos. For formal occasions, she can use the whole name: Maria Díaz Sanchez de Galdos. (And that's not including middle names!) Maria and José's children will use the last names of both parents: Galdos Díaz.

Maria and José may also receive a special title from young children or anyone who wants to show them respect. *Don* and *Doña* are similar to "Sir" and "Madam" in English. They are only used with first names, so our imaginary couple would be Doña Maria and Don José.

Although this system of names seems very complicated, Spaniards are used to it. It is a tradition, one of many in Spanish life. Despite the many changes in their society in recent years, most Spaniards still have strong roots in tradition and honor the customs of their society.

The Catholic Church is very important in Spanish life.
Rural churches are often social centers as well.

School Days

Every school day, thousands of Spanish students file into the classrooms of the University of Salamanca. For the most part, these young people could not be more modern. There are lots of blue jeans to be seen, many radios blaring rock music, and even an occasional streak of dyed-orange hair. In other words, it's a university scene that could be found almost anywhere in the world.

There is one difference, however. The university these students are attending is over 750 years old. Today's students walk along the same halls where young Spaniards discussed philosophy in the Middle Ages. They sit at desks carved with the initials of scholars who studied there during the sixteenth century. They visit classrooms where professors once lectured while members of the Inquisition watched from the back of the room.

Old Schools, New Schools

Students at the University of Salamanca may wander through historic halls, but most Spanish students have exactly the opposite experience—their schools are likely to be extremely new. That's because Spain is opening more and more schools every year. Some are in buildings that were once convents, factories, or even castles. Others are in modern buildings whose paint is hardly dry when the first children arrive to meet their new teachers.

There are two types of schools in Spain, state-run and private. Most private schools are sponsored by the Catholic Church and are usually either all-male or all-female. State schools generally accept both boys and girls. Tuition at all schools is paid by the government, although children in private schools must pay extra fees. This can be quite expensive. At one private school, for example, extra fees are charged for medical exams, sports, teaching materials, information bulletins, insurance, PTA dues, a swimming pool, testing materials, and maintenance of equipment.

No matter which type of school they attend, all children must buy their own books. Texts are not lent out and returned at the end of the term as they are in most United States schools. Grants are sometimes given to students who cannot afford the cost of books.

Most young children wear uniforms to school. Boys usually wear a one-piece overall that is blue, brown, or white. Some boys wear pants with a belted smock on top. Girls dress in pinafores, apronlike garments made of plain or striped light-colored cloth. Sometimes the children wear embroidered name badges on the front of the uniforms. Like children everywhere, Spanish kids like to play, and their uniforms show it. September's neat, spotless outfits are usually fairly ragged by June.

First- and Second-Stage Schools

Currently, Spanish law requires children to attend school from ages 6 to 16. However, some parents send their sons and daughters to nursery school at the age of three, and even more enroll their children at four or five. As in American nursery schools, the children paint, work with clay, and learn some numbers and letters. Now that *El Barrio Sesamo* (*Sesame Street*) is on Spanish TV, many children come to school already able to count and name the letters of the alphabet.

At the age of six, students begin the *Primera Etapa* (First Stage) of their official schooling. This lasts until age 12. During these years, the children stay in one room with the same teacher all day. From ages 13 to 16, the children are in the *Segunda Etapa* (Second Stage). Though they remain in the same building, they now change teachers for each subject.

Spanish children spend a lot more time in school than do American children. In a typical Spanish school of the first or second stage, students arrive around 8:30 A.M. They play in an enclosed patio (like a schoolyard) until the bell rings at 9:00. Then the children form lines and follow their

Young children often attend nursery school, where they paint, draw, and learn numbers and letters.

teachers into the building. They have classes until about 11:00 and then a half-hour outdoor recess. Many children eat a small snack before returning to class. Soon it's time for lunch. Students who live nearby go home for lunch. Those who stay in the building are served a hot meal in the school's dining room. A typical menu might include rice, fish, salad, and cookies; or beans, potatoes, meatballs, and fruit. Then the children are given games to amuse themselves with until their classmates return from home. A popular pastime is table soccer, which has a board as a

Spanish children study subjects similar to those in American schools. These students are working on a math problem with their teacher.

field and little players mounted on long, metal rods. One child stands at each end of the board and moves the players up and down the field.

In the afternoon the students study for two more hours, with a half-hour break. At 5:30, most children head home for the day; those who have fallen behind in their work stay for an extra hour of instruction. As if this schedule were not long enough, there is also a half-day of school on Saturdays!

Most of the subjects Spanish children study are similar to those in American schools. Naturally, Spanish replaces English. Schools in provinces where other languages are spoken, such as Catalonia and the Basque provinces, also teach their province's language. Second-stage children take a foreign language (usually English or French) and may have a course called pre-technology. In pre-technology, the students learn to make models, to construct simple machines, and to do craftwork. In both state and private schools, all pupils study religion or a course in ethics. Students also take gym, which includes sports such as volleyball, basketball, and soccer, as well as first-aid instruction, hiking, and map-reading. Unfortunately, most Spanish schools are built without playing fields, so the children must play sports in their school's patio.

The chart on page 114 shows one 16-year-old's schedule for the last year of the second stage.

Bachillerato

At the age of 16, students who do not intend to go on to college may attend a technical school. There, they learn skills such as auto mechanics and prepare for a noncollege career. Precollege students enter *bachillerato*, which is a type of high school. At this stage, there are no uniforms, and everyone must pay tuition in both state and private schools.

During the four years of bachillerato, a student may take courses in Spanish, math, foreign languages, history,

	9:00–10:00	10:00–11:00	11:00–11:30	11:30–12:30	3:00–4:00	4:00–4:30	4:30–5:30
MONDAY	Spanish	Math	Recess	Foreign Language (English)	Science	Recess	Art
TUESDAY	Math	Spanish	Recess	Social Studies	Gym	Recess	Gym
WEDNESDAY	Spanish	Math	Recess	Foreign Language (English)	Religion	Recess	Social Studies
THURSDAY	Math	Spanish	Recess	Religion	Science	Recess	Art
FRIDAY	Spanish	Math	Recess	Foreign Language (English)	Gym	Recess	Social Studies
SATURDAY	Music, Drama, or Pre-technology				No School		
SUNDAY	No school all day						

science, religion, gym, social studies, crafts, and home economics.

Grading Systems

The illustration on page 115 shows a report card for a ten-year-old Spanish child in the first stage. As you see, teachers do not use the letter-grade system. Instead, a child may receive the following marks: *Muy Deficiente* (very unsatisfactory), *Insuficiente* (unsatisfactory), *Suficiente* (satisfactory), *Bien* (good), *Notable* (very good), and *Sobresaliente* (outstanding). On this report card, Vanesa Moles was rated outstanding in Spanish, math, science, and

BOLETIN DE EVALUACION FINAL	ALUMNO							No. AL	CLASE	CURSO	SECC
	MOLES DEFIOR, VANESA							39	39	5	A
CENTRO	CORRESPONDENCIA							ENSEÑANZA			
COLEGIO PUBLICO "SIERRA NEVADA" GRANADA 6908								C. ME			
								No. MATRICULA			
								FECHA			
								21-6-83			

MATERIAS	CALIFICACION FINAL	EVALUACIONES						PENDIENTES DE RECUPERAR
		1	2	3	4	5	6	
LENGUA CASTELLANA	SOBRESALIENTE							
MATEMATICAS	SOBRESALIENTE							
CIENCIAS NATURALEZA	SOBRESALIENTE							
CIENCIAS SOCIALES	SOBRESALIENTE							
ENS. RELIGIOSA-ETICA	NOTABLE							
EDUCACION ARTISTICA	NOTABLE							
EDUCACION FISICA	BIEN							

CALIFICACION GLOBAL DEL CURSO   SOBRESALIENTE

OBSERVACIONES DE LA JUNTA DE EVALUACION

*LAS MATERIAS SEÑALADAS CON ASTERISCO INDICAN PENDIENTES DE RECUPERAR   LAS MATERIAS SEÑALADAS CON SIGNO + HAN SIDO RECUPERADAS

social studies; very good in religion and art; and good in physical education.

The same system of marks continues into bachillerato. In some schools, students receive progress reports every week, with formal marks given after final exams at the end of the year. The same final exam is given in every school of the province. This is to make sure that all Spanish schools follow the required course of instruction. Although no one likes finals, Spanish students have no reason to be afraid at the end of the year. Children who fail their final exams are not left back. Instead, they are given extra work over the summer and during the regular school year. Then they take their exams again.

Going to the University

After bachillerato, students who plan to go on to college enroll in a one-year preparation course. They take the same subjects the bachillerato offers but on a higher level. They may also take a course that introduces various career fields such as law, medicine, or education. At the end of the year, there is a final. Students who fail may take one or two more years of college preparation until they are ready for the university.

How would you like to go to a school with 130,000 other young people? That's how many students attend the University of Madrid. Over 50,000 are registered at the Central University of Barcelona. However, not all Spanish universities are that large. Some "small" Spanish colleges have only 5,000 students.

With numbers like these, it is clear that Spanish professors cannot get to know every one of their students. They may have classes with as many as 1,000 young men and women registered! University teachers rely on lectures and readings to present their ideas, and final exams to check on their students' success.

Some students live at home and travel daily to class,

College students like these young women will receive a Licenciatura after five years of advanced study.

but others live in dormitories or *colegios*—residences for students. The colegio provides the personal contact that the university classes do not. Students who live there study with each other and with their houseparents, who try to make the colegio a kind of "home away from home" for their charges. Colegios sponsor concerts, parties, lectures, and clubs for their students. Most colegios have a café where students can unwind after classes.

For those students who live out in the country and can

not attend classes at all, the government's department of education has recently begun long-distance colleges. These students receive lessons in the mail or by way of radio, television, or computer.

The university course lasts five years, after which a *Licenciatura* is awarded. Students can also receive a lesser degree after three years. Those who wish to continue beyond the Licenciatura can study for a *Doctorado* (doctorate), which takes two years to complete.

In the past, students who wished to study advanced or very technical subjects often had to go to other countries because the schools in Spain were not good. The Spanish government was aware of this problem. In fact, better education has been the goal of all the Spanish governments since before the Spanish Civil War. At the beginning of this century, only the children of wealthy Spaniards were well educated. Most peasants could not read or write at all. The Republic opened thousands of new schools, but even this was not enough to provide places for all Spanish children. Also, many children who did have a school nearby were unable to attend, even though their presence was required by law. Their families were so poor that the labors of everyone were needed just to survive.

The Franco government continued the effort to improve education. By 1952, seventy-two percent of Spain's school-age children were being educated. Twenty years later the number had jumped to 96 percent. Today nearly all eligible children are in school. The schools themselves have also been improved. Future Spanish engineers, architects, doctors, and other professionals can now find all the training they need right in their own country.

BULLFIGHTS AND BASKETBALL

The sun blazes on a golden circle of sand. In the center of the circle, a man dressed in tight-fitting pants and a jeweled jacket stands holding a cape. Fifty yards away is a huge bull. Quietly the man twirls the cape. The creature, and everyone in the crowd, watches carefully. Suddenly the bull charges! The crowd rises to its feet as the matador faces death in the form of a thousand pounds of muscle, two sharp horns, and lightning hooves. Cheers explode: The matador steps aside at the very last second, and the bull runs harmlessly past.

The roots of bullfighting go deep into Iberian history. Even the cave artists of Altamira painted bulls, and until recently, the bullfight was every Spaniard's favorite pastime. Children using kitchen towels for capes took turns playing bull and matador. Successful bullfighters were national heroes, and newspapers reviewed each matador's performance. Long lines formed to buy the cheap *sol* (sunny) and the expensive *sombra* (shady) seats for every fight. Today the popularity of bullfighting is lessening somewhat. Many bullfights are now attended more by tourists than by Spaniards.

One thing never changes, however. The bullfight is

Although not as popular as they once were, bullfights still attract many spectators. Here, a bull charges the matador.

still surrounded by a great deal of ceremony. Each fight begins with the matadores and their teams parading around the ring. A trumpet sounds and the bullfighters bow to the president of the arena. From his high seat, he throws down the key that unlocks the bulls' pen. The ring is cleared and the bull enters.

Picadores on horseback and *bandarilleros* on foot chase and wound the bull. Finally, the matador strides into the ring, and the real drama begins. The weakened bull charges again and again as the bullfighter encourages the animal to come closer and closer. Sometimes the bull manages to hurt the bullfighter with its horns. Usually, though, the human wins. At the end of the fight, the matador drives a sword through the bull's neck and into his heart, and the match is over.

Arena officials judge the matador's performance. If the matador has fought well, he or she may be awarded an ear, a hoof, or the tail of the dead bull. The crowd also shows its approval by throwing presents into the ring. After a good fight, flowers, hats, sausages, and even sweaters come showering down from the stands.

Some people are horrified by bullfights. They are angered by animals being wounded and killed in the sport, and they believe that people who enjoy such a show must be very cruel. Yet bullfighting fans view their sport differently. To them the struggle between a human and an enormously powerful animal is beautiful. Although the bull nearly always loses, the animal's bravery and willingness to fight earn it the respect of the crowd. In the same way, the matador's courage and grace are important—not simply the fact that he or she kills the bull.

Soccer and Other Sports

Bullfights are not as popular in Spain as they used to

Soccer is popular wih Spaniards of all ages.

be because many Spaniards have transferred their attention to soccer. Soccer, which is called *futbol* in Spanish, is played in front of sellout crowds in every city. Even the tiniest village has a soccer team, and on weekends neighboring towns play each other. It is not unusual for the entire village to watch a game, probably while enjoying a picnic lunch. The proud family of a star player may even use the team photo as a Christmas card! At World Cup time, everyone clusters around television sets to cheer Spain's national team.

Another popular Spanish sport is *jai alai*, or *pelota*, which is played with a hard ball and a small, shallow basket called a *cesta*. Jai alai originated in the Basque province. It is said to be the fastest and most exhausting game in the world. Players catch the ball in their cestas and fling the ball against a wall. The other team must catch the lightning-fast rebound. Professionals play jai alai in a court; children often play the game using the side of their school or church as a backstop.

Basketball also has many fans in Spain. In recent years several teams from the National Basketball Association (NBA) have played in Spain to sellout crowds. "Footing"—running—is becoming more popular, too. An annual marathon is held in Madrid with thousands of runners taking part. The international success of tennis star Arantxa Sánchez Vicario, cyclist Miguel Indurain, and

Jai alai is a fast-paced game requiring great skill.

golfer Seve Ballesteros has made these sports more attractive to Spanish youngsters as well.

Boys and girls very seldom play together in Spain. The traditional male and female roles are still strong, though many more activities are now open to girls. Girls participate in volleyball, basketball, and track. For the most part, bullfighting, soccer, and jai alai remain all-male, although

Spain now has a few female bullfighters. Young girls also play a kind of jump rope with an elastic cord and a hopscotch game with soda bottle caps. Both boys and girls ride bikes on the streets or in their schoolyards.

The youngest children, both boys and girls, enjoy games like cops and robbers. The "cops" chase the "robbers," and after the arrest is made, the roles are reversed. Spanish kids also play tag, hide-and-seek, and board games like Monopoly and Parcheesi. Just recently, video and computer games have become the rage!

Spanish interest in sports reached a new height in 1992, when the summer Olympics were held in Barcelona. An international audience, including Spaniards from every region of the country, watched great athletes such as sprinter Carl Lewis and swimmer Janet Evans compete. One young man was the subject of extra attention. Prince Felipe, heir to the Spanish throne, was a member of the Spanish yachting team. Prince Felipe carried his nation's flag during the opening ceremony, which included a pageant representing episodes from the history of Spain. Perhaps the most thrilling moment was when a Spanish archer shot a flaming arrow clear across the huge Olympic Stadium to light the Olympic torch.

An important Spanish pastime is the *paseo*—a long, slow walk through the center of town. There people meet neighbors and friends, exchange the latest gossip, and

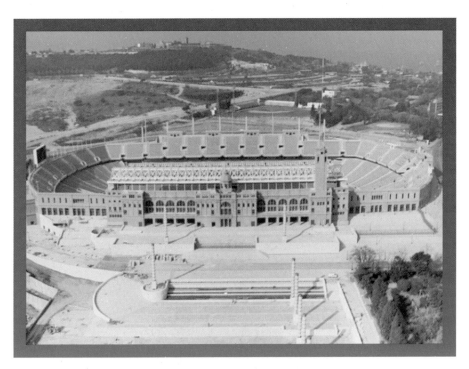

Olympic Stadium in Barcelona was the site of many events at the 1992 Olympics.

show off new clothes. Married couples stroll arm in arm, teenagers flirt with each other, and young children race up and down ahead of their parents.

Late afternoon is the most common time for a paseo, and many people also go out on Sunday mornings after Mass. In Madrid, Sunday walkers may wander through the *rastro*, an open-air flea market. The rastro is famous for selling anything and everything: A pile of fashion magazines from 1889 may sit on top of new sponges and kitchen towels. Bargain hunters have a wonderful time at the rastro.

Cafés, *Tertulias,* and Discos

No one can walk all the time, and one of the best parts of a paseo is a stop in a café. Spaniards love to watch what's going on, so in all but the coldest weather, cafés put tables and chairs outdoors. There, customers may sit for hours, watching the paseo and sipping a cup of coffee or a glass of wine. No waiter will annoy them by asking them to order more—in Spain it is expected that life goes on at a leisurely pace.

In the corners of some cafés, people gather in the evening for a *tertulia*. A tertulia is an informal "talking club." The members never ask to join and never plan when they are going to meet next. They seem to drift together every so often. Yet, tertulias can become permanent institutions. One tertulia in Madrid met once a week for 30 years! The topics discussed in a tertulia depend on the members. Farmers are likely to argue about the price of olive oil or the best method for fertilizing orange trees. Business executives and students may tackle politics, religion, or the weather. Some tertulias change subjects each week; others are organized according to interest. Visitors to the café may sometimes choose between several types of tertulias.

In the Basque country, many "talking clubs" are also "eating clubs." Basque men (never the women) go to club-houses in the evening to cook a big, fancy meal. Every

Shoppers can find anything and everything at the rastro in Madrid.

member takes turns doing the dishwashing chores, and the cook is a different man each night. No matter how much the group enjoys a particular meal, every member is sure that his recipe is clearly better than the one the cook used!

Younger Spaniards are more likely to be found in a discotheque than in a tertulia or an eating club. It has been said that Spain has more night clubs than any other European country. The crowds begin to gather a few hours after supper (around midnight), and they dance until three or four in the morning. American and British rock-and-roll music are the favorites, although Spanish pop tunes are also played.

Television, Theater, and Movies

Spaniards who are not out on a paseo or arguing in a tertulia are likely to be home watching television. Spanish television broadcasts in Castilian, Catalan, Galician, and Euskera.

What do Spaniards watch? Just about all the same kinds of programs Americans do: There are news shows and information shows, sporting events (mostly soccer, but also important bullfights), and entertainment. Spanish TV also broadcasts many concerts of Spanish music as well as Catholic Mass every Sunday. As in the United States, the most popular shows are often movies that appeared in

Cafés are excellent spots for meeting friends or watching the paseo.

theaters a few years earlier. Many of the movies and TV
shows are imported from other countries, but the sound-
track is translated into Spanish. TV listings may include
such programs as *Sesame Street*, *Barney*, and *Beverly
Hills 90210.*

Going out to the movies is also a favorite Spanish pastime. In cities the theaters resemble those of the United
States. In small villages the meeting room of the town hall
or an open-air tent may become a theater on weekends.
Spanish filmmakers and actors have become increasingly
famous around the world. Director Pedro Almodóvar and
actors Antonio Banderas and Victoria Abril are three of the
most popular Spaniards working in film.

All large cities and many small ones also have live
theater performances. Actors present the great classics of
Spanish theater as well as modern plays from Spain and
other countries. Ticket prices for plays are fairly low;
students who have very little spending money often ask for
a seat "in heaven." That's the last row or two near the
ceiling of the theater, close to the sky!

The popularity of the theater is just one example of
what can also be seen in the Spanish devotion to sports,
tertulias, paseos, and other pastimes: Spaniards know how
to enjoy life!

ADVENTURE IN AMERICA

One of the first Spanish immigrants to the New World started a very long walk one day. Álvar Núñez Cabeza de Vaca was shipwrecked in the Gulf of Mexico in 1528. When he came ashore on Galveston Island, near the coast of Texas, he was captured by the Karakawa Indians. The Karakawa made Cabeza de Vaca their slave, but he soon gained a reputation among them as a medicine man. After seven years with the Karakawas, Cabeza de Vaca escaped and began to walk west. Many months later, he reached a Spanish mission in Mexico. Cabeza de Vaca had traveled on foot across half of what is now the United States!

This journey was only one of the adventures that America had in store for the Spaniards. When Cabeza de Vaca returned to Spain, he told everyone about "the seven cities of Cibola," which were said to be made of gold. Hernando De Soto heard these tales and decided to search for the treasure. De Soto traveled throughout the southeastern United States, taking many valuables along the way. One Indian chief gave him over 300 pounds of pearls! However, De Soto never found the golden cities. (And for good reason: They did not exist!)

Francisco de Coronado also set out to find Cibola, searching in what is now Arizona, New Mexico, Texas, and

Kansas. His expedition began in 1540 and included 300 soldiers, 700 American Indian slaves, 1,000 horses, and many other animals and supplies. Coronado did find a "Cibola," but not the one he had been dreaming about for so long. Instead of golden cities, he discovered seven small Zuni Indian villages, where the inhabitants' most valuable possessions were straw huts and corn.

Although these Spaniards' journeys through America did not turn out the way they expected, their expeditions were not failures. Cabeza de Vaca, De Soto, and Coronado were the first Europeans to explore the area of the southern United States. They claimed all the land they traveled through for Spain. This added vast colonies to the Spanish Empire—colonies whose natural resources were even more valuable than the legendary treasures of Cibola could ever have been.

Of course, the land claimed by these explorers, as well as most of the treasure and resources sent back to Spain, belonged to the American Indians. Many times the Spaniards fought bloody battles with the native peoples to get this wealth. Whole cultures such as those of the Aztecs of Mexico and the Incas of Peru were destroyed by Spanish troops, who were sometimes helped by the native rivals of those cultures. American Indians were killed or enslaved, in many cases, and cities were leveled so that new settlements could be built in their places.

Spanish Settlements

As Hernando De Soto and Francisco de Coronado traveled throughout the South, members of their expeditions stayed behind from time to time, creating many small settlements. De Soto himself founded Tampa Bay, Florida.

In the West other Spanish immigrants were also colonizing California. Juan Rodríguez Cabrillo had explored and claimed the coasts of California and Oregon for Spain in 1542. However, no settlements were established in that territory for 200 years. Then a party of Spaniards traveled north from Mexico. A member of that group was Junípero Serra, a truly remarkable man.

Junípero Serra had been born on the island of Majorca in 1713. When he was 16, he entered a Catholic religious order and became a friar (brother). Twenty years later he sailed for the New World to bring the message of his faith to the American Indians. At first he worked in Mexico, but in 1769 he was sent to establish Catholic missions in California. Serra had a bad leg and walked with difficulty. In spite of this, he spent the next 15 years walking throughout the Southwest and West.

He first walked from Mexico to San Diego. There he built a church and started a small settlement. Then he walked north, founding a string of missions along the California coast. Each mission was one day's walk from the next. Other friars joined Serra, and eventually there

Father Junípero Serra founded many missions in California, including Mission San Carlos Borromeo at Carmel.

were 21 missions along a road that was named *El Camino Real*—the royal highway. Serra eventually became the head of his church in California. One of his duties was to travel from mission to mission on foot, visiting his priests and converts. Although no one has added it up, Serra may have put in as many miles as Cabeza de Vaca!

If you look at a modern map of the United States, you will see the names of settlements founded by Friar Serra and other Spanish immigrants. Many are named after saints—San Francisco, Saint Augustine, San Antonio, San Jose, Sante Fe, and hundreds more. Los Angeles, Monterey, Tucson, and Albuquerque are other Spanish settlements that grew into important American cities.

A Huge Minority

Spain kept control of much of the southern United States for about 300 years. Then in the nineteenth century, all of Spain's former lands in North America became part of the United States by treaty or sale. After the Spanish-American War in 1898, the United States took possession of Puerto Rico, Cuba, and the Philippines. Cuba and the Philippines eventually received their independence, but Puerto Rico became a commonwealth of the United States.

Many Puerto Ricans and other Latino people from South and Central America are descendants of the Spaniards who explored and settled the Western Hemisphere long ago. Their ancestors also include the native peoples and black slaves who were brought by the Spaniards to work in the colonies. Throughout the years many Latinos have immigrated to the United States. Their many accomplishments may be included in the list of contributions Spain has made to this country.

Immigration to the United States from Spain itself did not end in the colonial days. Throughout the nineteenth century, a few thousand Spaniards left their homeland and arrived in the United States each year. At the beginning of the twentieth century, the pressures that eventually led to the Spanish Civil War increased. Because of this, the number of Spanish immigrants jumped dramatically. Between 1870 and 1900 (a 30-year period), about 18,000 Spaniards came to the United States. During the next 30 years, over 125,000 immigrated to this country.

Quite a few of these new Americans came from the Basque country. Many Basques settled in the Great Basin, an area that includes parts of Utah, California, Oregon, Idaho, and Nevada. The immigrants often became shepherds or worked in other areas of the sheep industry. Today there are 10,000 to 15,000 people of Basque descent in the Great Basin. They have a "Sheepherders' Ball" and a Saint Ignatius Day picnic in Boise, Idaho, every year. (Saint Ignatius of Loyola was born in the Basque country.) Senator Paul Laxalt, who represents Nevada in the United States Congress, is of Basque descent.

Other Spanish immigrants have scattered throughout the United States. Often, these new Americans settle in the Latino neighborhoods of major cities. Although Spanish-speaking Americans come from many countries and have different cultures and customs, their common language unites them. In some areas, homesick Spanish Americans have formed clubs where they can enjoy some memories of

These boys and girls perform music at a Basque club in the United States.

emigrated from Spain—they are both victims of prejudice. In the minds of some Americans, all Spanish-speaking people are the same, and none are to be trusted. Prejudice has often been directed at immigrants. Throughout the history of the United States, each new group has faced some distrust and disapproval, especially if the group's numbers are large. Some Americans fear that the newcomers will take their jobs; others are simply baffled by the immigrants' foreign ways.

Palm Trees, Horses, and Oranges

In spite of this prejudice, the United States would be a much poorer country today without the contributions of Spanish Americans. In California, for example,

American Indians believed that the first Spanish explorers they saw were half-human and half-animal. They had never seen a horse and rider before!)

The early Spanish colonists also brought new types of farming tools to America, and they taught other Americans their methods of caring for sheep and cattle. This had an effect on our language, too. Many of the English words that cowboys use today originally came from Spanish, including *lariat*, *lasso*, *bronco*, *corral*, *rodeo*, *chaps*, *cinch*, *ranch*, and *stampede*. The hard-working Spaniards also introduced another word to English when they rested from their labors—*siesta*!

Spain has also influenced American cooking. Many people have sampled sangría, paella, and Spanish omelettes. Found mostly in Louisiana, Creole cooking is a mixture of Spanish and French styles, passed down by the colonists who settled there long ago. A quick drive through southern California or the Southwest reveals another Spanish contribution. The adobe bricks, inner patios, and iron balconies of many houses are just like those found in the South of Spain.

Some Famous Spanish Americans

In the United States Capitol building in Washington, D.C., each state is allowed to erect statues of its two most honored citizens. One of the statues representing California is of Junípero Serra. Serra is not the only Spanish immigrant from that time to achieve fame in the United States. Pedro Menéndez de Avilés, a member of a noble Asturian family, ran away from home at the age of 14. He became a sailor and fought in a war between France and Spain. In 1565 the king of Spain sent Menéndez de Avilés to Florida. There he founded Saint Augustine, which is the oldest city in the United States. Other Spaniards founded and named many other cities in the American South and Southwest.

In more recent times, José Greco became the most famous flamenco dancer in the United States. Greco, whose mother was Spanish, was born in Italy in 1918. When he was very young, his family moved to America. Greco became a professional dancer and a real flamenco artist. A critic once commented that Greco danced ". . . as if he were awfully angry at the floor!" Xavier Cugat, who was born in Barcelona, Spain, in 1900, moved to Cuba when he was a boy. He eventually formed a dance band and brought many Americans their first taste of Latin dancing. Pablo Casals, another native Catalonian, fled Spain during the Spanish Civil War and eventually settled in Puerto Rico. Casals was one of the greatest cellists in the world; he died in 1973. The writer Juan Ramón Jiménez also left Spain for Puerto Rico when the

*José Greco, here with his partner, Nana Lorca, popularized
flamenco dancing throughout the world.*

*Born in Madrid, singer Julio Iglesias today lives in Miami, Florida.
His concerts are sold out wherever he performs.*

Republicans lost the Spanish Civil War. Jiménez's most famous work is *Platero and I*, a wonderful story about a little donkey and his master. Jiménez won the Nobel Prize in literature in 1956. Luis Buñuel, a filmmaker, was also a war refugee. He settled in the United States in 1938 and later moved to Mexico. Another Spanish American, Severo Ochoa, was born in Luarca, Spain, but later moved to the United States. He won the Nobel Prize in medicine in 1959 for his work with nucleic acids. Julio Iglesias, a singer popular all over the world, but originally from Spain, today lives in Miami, Florida.

Of course, there are many, many people of Spanish descent involved in every aspect of life in America. The United States has benefitted greatly from their hard work and their unsung contributions to American life.

There is an old Spanish proverb, "Whoever says 'Spain' says everything." There is a tremendous amount of variety packed into Spain's small area of land. Its people reflect this variety and bring a rich culture and a proud heritage with them when they adopt the United States as their home.

Appendix A

Castilian Spanish: A Guide to Pronunciation

Castilian, the type of Spanish spoken in Spain, differs somewhat in pronunciation from the Spanish spoken in North, South, and Central America. Spanish is rather regular in pronunciation, and almost every letter in each word is pronounced. Below is a chart showing the sounds that letters generally have in Spanish.

a   as in *papa*

b   hard *(bike)* at the beginning of a word;
      soft *(table)* within a word

c   as in *cat*; but before *e* and *i*, sounds like the *th* in *think*

ch   as in *chow*

d   as in *dawn* when at the beginning or end of a word; but sounds like the *th* in *that* when within a word

e   as in *they*

f   as in *fat*

g   as in *gas* when it begins a word or comes before the letters *a*, *o*, *u*, or after *n*; as a breathy *h* sound when it appears before the letters *e* or *i* or in the middle of a word

h   is silent

i   as in *police*

j   as a breathy *h* sound

k   as in *kernel*; only found in adopted non-Spanish words

l   as in *late*

ll   as the *y* in *year*

m   as in *more*

n   as in *not*; when it appears before the letters *b*, *v*, *p*, or *f*, it has an *m* sound

ñ   has a *nyuh* sound

o   as in *flow*

p   as in *open*

q   always used with *u*; *qu* as in *quite*

r   pronounced as the *tt* in *pretty* when within a word; rolled *(rr)* when it begins a word, appears as a double *r*, or comes before the letters *l*, *n*, or *s*

s   as in *sun*; but sounds like the *s* in *pose* when it comes before the letters *b*, *v*, *d*, *m*, *n*, *l*, *g*, or *r*

t   as in *stupid*

u   as in *ruler*

v   pronounced either as a *b (baby)* or as a regular *v* as in English.

w   not used in Spanish

x   as in *ax*; but sometimes it has a *gss* sound before a consonant

y   as in *year*

z   as the *th* in *think*

Special letter combinations

ai   as the *i* in *life*

au   as the *ow* in *towel*

ei   as the *ay* in *way*

ia   as *eeyah*

io   as *eeyoh*

iu   as *eeyuh*

oi   as the *oy* in *toy*

ua   as the *wa* in *watch*

ui   as the *we* in *week*

ue   as the *we* in *wet*

uo   as the *wo* in *woke*

Appendix B

Spanish Embassies and Consulates in the United States and Canada

The embassies and consulates of Spain would be glad to help you learn more about Spain. They can recommend books and articles and direct you to information about traveling in their country.

U.S. Embassy and Consulates

Boston, Massachusetts
Consulate General of Spain
545 Boylston St., Suite 803
Boston, MA 02116
Phone (617) 536-2506

Chicago, Illinois
Consulate General of Spain
180 N. Michigan Ave., Suite 1500
Chicago, IL 60601
Phone (312) 782-4588

Houston, Texas
Consulate General of Spain
1800 Bering Drive, Suite 660
Houston, TX 77057
Phone (713) 783-6200

Los Angeles, California
Consulate General of Spain
5055 Wilshire Blvd., Suite 960
Los Angeles, CA 90048
Phone (213) 938-0158

Miami, Florida
Consulate General of Spain
2655 Le Jeune Rd., Suite 203
Coral Gables, FL 33134
Phone (305) 446-5511

New Orleans, Louisiana
Consulate General of Spain
2102 World Trade Center
2 Canal St.
New Orleans, LA 70130
Phone (504) 525-4951

New York, New York
Consulate General of Spain
150 E. 58th St., 30th floor
New York, NY 10155
Phone (212) 355-4080

San Francisco, California
Consulate General of Spain
1405 Sutter St.
San Francisco, CA 94109
Phone (415) 922-2995

Washington, D.C.
Embassy of Spain
2375 Pennsylvania Ave.
Washington, D.C. 20009
Phone (202) 728-2330

Canadian Embassy and Consulate

Montreal, Quebec
Consulate General of Spain
1 Westmount Sq., Suite 1456
Montreal, Quebec H3Z 2P9
Phone (514) 935-5235

Ottawa, Ontario
Embassy of Spain
350 E. Sparks St., Suite 802
Ottawa, Ontario K1R 7S8
Phone (613) 237-2193

Glossary

Armada (ahr MAH dah)—fleet of Spanish ships defeated by the British navy in 1588

bachillerato (bah chee ye RAH toh)—college preparatory high school

banderillero (bahn de ree YE roh)—bullfighter who challenges a bull on foot and weakens it by pushing sharp sticks into its neck

Barrio Sesamo (BAH rree oh SE sah moh), **El**—Spanish version of the TV program *Sesame Street*

belén (be LEN)—Christmas decoration consisting of a stable with figures of people and animals in it

bien (bee EN)—good; a grade like a *C* in American schools

bocadillo (boh kah DEE yoh)—small stuffed snack roll

bota (BOH tah)—leather wine sack

Carlanco (kahr LAHN koh)—monster in Spanish fairy tales

cena (THE nah)—supper, served around 10:00 P.M.

cesta (THES tah)—shallow catching basket used in the game of jai alai

chateo (chah TE oh)—Spanish custom of dropping in on a number of restaurants to eat appetizers and drink wine

chato (CHAH toh)—small glass of wine

churro (CHOO rroh)—thin, deep-fried doughnut

Cibola (thee BOH lah)—legendary place where there were seven wealthy cities

colegio (koh LE hee oh)—college residence hall

comido (koh MEE doh) dinner, the most important Spanish meal of the day, eaten in mid-afternoon

conquistador (kohn KEES tah dor)—"conqueror"; term used for the Spanish explorers in the New World

copla (KOH plah)—short poem set to music

cortado (kor TAH doh)—"cut"; used to describe expresso with a little milk in it

Covadonga (koh vah DOHN guh)—cave where Pelayo and his army fought at the beginning of the Reconquest

doctorado (dahk toh RAH doh)—university degree granted after seven years of study

Don (dohn)—title of respect for a man

Doña (DOH nyah)—title of respect for a woman

Euskera (e oos KE rah)—ancient Basque language

expresso (eks PRE soh)—strong coffee made by quickly forcing boiling water through powderlike dark coffee grounds

Fallas (FAH yahs)—festival in Valencia where huge papier-mâché figures are paraded and burned

Feria (FE ree ah)—festival of Seville

Finisterre (fee nees TE rre)—Latin for "the end of the earth"

flamenco (flah MEN koh)—Spanish dance featuring quick, clicking steps and hand-clapping

Hispania (ees PAH nee ah)—Roman name for Spain

Hormiguita (or mee GEE tah)—"Little Ant"; Spanish fairy-tale character

Inquisición (een kee see thee OHN)—religious court in Spain that tried to purify the Catholic religion

insuficiente (een soo fee see EN te)—"unsatisfactory"; grade like a *D* in American schools

jai alai (HYE ah lye)—fast-paced game played against a wall, using a hard rubber ball and catching baskets

jota (HOH tah)—folk dance of Aragon

licenciatura (lee sen see ah TOO rrah)—university degree given after five years of study

Macarena (mah kah RE nah), **La**—famous statue in Seville of Our Lady of Hope that is paraded through the city streets

mañana (mahn YAH nah)—word meaning "tomorrow"

matador (mah tah DOR)—bullfighter who alone kills the bull at the end of a fight

merienda (me ree EN dah)—late-afternoon snack

Miguelete (mee ge LE te), **El**—eight-sided bell tower in Valencia

Moors (moorz)—Arab people of northwest Africa who ruled Spain for seven hundred years

Moriscos (moh REES kohs)—descendants of the Moors who changed their religion from Islam to Roman Catholic

muy deficiente (mwee de fee see YEN te)—"very unsatisfactory"; grade like an *F* in American schools

notable (noh TAH ble)—"very good"; grade like a *B* in American schools

paella (pah E yah)—dish of saffron rice, vegetables, meat, and seafood

paseo (pah SE oh)—traditional Spanish evening walk

patria chica (PAH tree ah CHEE kah)—"little homeland"; phrase referring to the region where a Spaniard was born and raised

pelota (pe LOH tah)—another name for jai alai

picador (pee kah DOR)—bullfighter who fights a bull on horseback

porrón (poh RROHN)—glass wine pitcher with a long spout

Prado (PRAH doh) **Museum**—large art museum in Madrid

Primera Etapa (pree ME rah e TAH pah)—"first stage"; schools for children ages six through twelve

Puerta del Sol (PWER tah del SOHL), **La**—"Gate of the Sun"; plaza in Madrid

rastro (RAHS troh)—open-air market of Madrid

Ratón Pérez (rah TOHN PE reth)—"Perez the Mouse";
Spanish fairy-tale character

Romería del Rocío (roh meh REE ah del roh THEE oh)—
Andalusian festival honoring Our Lady of the Dew

saeta (sah E tah)—"arrow (of prayer)"; short, sad song
sung during solemn Holy Week processions

sangría (sahn GREE ah)—wine and fruit punch

sardana (sahr DAH nah)—folk dance of Catalonia

Segunda Etapa (se GOON dah e TAH pah)—"second
stage"; schools for children ages 13 to 16

sobresaliente (soh bre sah lee EN te)—"outstanding";
grade like an *A* in American schools

sol (sohl)—sun; sunny

solea (soh LE ah)—type of flamenco

sombra (SOHM brah)—shade, shady

tapa (TAH pah)—Spanish appetizer

tertulia (ter too LEE ah)—talking club that meets in a bar
or café

tortilla española (tor TEE yah es pahn YOH lah)—potato
and egg omelette

tuna (TOO nah)—group of young men that serenades
young women

turrón (too RROHN)—hard candy eaten at Christmas

zarzuela (thahr THWE lah)—Spanish opera, often funny,
with spoken dialogue

SELECTED BIBLIOGRAPHY

Alvarado, Manuel. *Spain*. London: The Bookwright Press, 1989.

Bristow, Richard. *We Live in Spain*. London: The Bookwright Press, 1984.

Christian, Rebecca. *Cooking the Spanish Way*. Minneapolis: Lerner Publications, 1982.

Cross, Esther and Wilbur. *Spain*. Chicago: The Children's Press, 1985.

Crow, John A. *Spain, the Root and the Flower*. 3rd ed. Berkeley: University of Calfornia Press, 1985.

Graham, Robert. *Spain: A Nation Comes of Age*. New York: St. Martin's Press, 1984.

Miller, Arthur. *Spain*. New York: Chelsea House, 1989.

Seth, Ronald. *Let's Visit Spain*. London: Burke, 1984.

Shubert, Adrian. *The Land and People of Spain*. New York: HarperCollins, 1992.

INDEX

ABOUT THE AUTHOR

Geraldine Woods fell in love with Spain the first time she traveled there and has since returned several times to visit family friends and to live there for brief periods. Her familiarity with this sunny land inspired her to write *Spain: Gateway to Europe*.

Ms. Woods has published many books for children on a variety of subjects, sometimes sharing the author billing with her husband, Harold. Among her books are *Bill Cosby: Making America Laugh and Learn*, *Equal Justice: A Biography of Sandra Day O'Connor*, and *Jim Henson: From Puppets to Muppets*. She is a teacher and lives with her family in New York City.